CW00422287

Android Tablets Ti_J

A How-To Tutorial for an...

Edward Jones

© 17 December 2013 by Jones-Mack Technology Services of Charlotte, NC.

Digital rights provided by agreement to Amazon Digital Services, Inc.

Print rights provided by agreement to CreateSpace (an Amazon Company).

£6.99

Nov. 2015

INTRODUCTION

Welcome to the Android Tablets Tips, Tricks, and Traps edition of this author's popular *Tips, Tricks, and Traps* guides, this edition written specifically for all Android tablets. Android tablets are handheld tablet-sized computers (typically measuring 7 to 10 inches in diagonal screen size) that run the phenomenally popular Android operating system developed by Google. There are literally hundreds of thousands of apps available for your tablet through the Google PlayStore, as well as through other sources on the internet. Whether you received your tablet as a gift or were sufficiently impressed by its feature set to shell out the funds needed for purchase, you now have a powerful and functional computer in your hands. And however you came into possession of your tablet, you probably have unanswered questions about its operation, or would just love to get the most out of your new tablet.

In this comprehensive guide, you'll learn tips (ways to effectively use your Android tablet), tricks (ways to improve the operation of your Android tablet), and traps (things to avoid to prevent problems while using your Android tablet). You will learn-

- How to get around within the Android-based user interface (meaning, what you see on the screen) more efficiently

- How to make your Android tablet your own, customizing its display and operation for fastest and easiest use
- How to find THOUSANDS of FREE (as in, 'zero dollars and zero cents') apps, books, songs, and other digital content
- How you can download YouTube videos to your Android tablet
- Suggested apps that no Android tablet owner should be without

You will learn all of the above and more, with *Android Tablets Tips, Tricks, and Traps: A How-To Tutorial for Android Tablets* as a part of your library. Read on, and learn 100% of what you need to know to get the most out of your Android tablet!

Table of Contents

Chapter 1: Android Tablets Out of the Box

Welcome to *Android Tablets Tips, Tricks, and Traps: A How-To Tutorial for Android Tablets*. Chances are high that your new Android-based tablet computer did not ship with much in the way of documentation, since device manufacturers worldwide appear to be shortchanging consumers in the area of user manuals. If that applies to you, you've come to the right place, and you can consider this publication to be the manual that should have been packed with your new tablet! There are things that you can do to make your Android tablet work best for you, and teaching you these topics is precisely what this book is about.

This book looks at three categories in every chapter: *tips*, *tricks*, and *traps*.

Tips are techniques that make things easier in terms of use, in a particular area.

Tricks are techniques that change the operation of your Android tablet in a particular area, often providing capabilities or performance improvements that just were not there out of the box.

Traps are "gotchas," things to watch out for, that can cause problems.

Android tablet setup

Set up your Android tablet now if it is fresh out of the box. If you've just opened the box containing your Android tablet, you'll need to turn it on and set it up before you can start using your tablet.

After you open the box and remove the usual paraphernalia that accompanies any sophisticated electronic device these days, you'll find yourself left with the following (besides the tablet itself, of course):

- A USB cable that you'll use to connect the tablet to a wall charger, or to a computer

- A wall charger. This may come in two parts, depending on your model of tablet and country of residence. If there are two parts, the larger of the two is the charger, and the smaller matches electrical sockets used in your country.

- Warranty paperwork, and typically, some sort of 'quick start' or 'read me first" documentation

- Depending on your model of tablet, you may also find a pair of "earbud"-style earphones packaged with your tablet

First things first: the very first step you should take with your new Android tablet fresh out of the box is to fully charge the built-in battery. Insert the USB (the wider) end of the cable into the wall charger, and insert the remaining end of the cable into the connector on the tablet that matches the shape of the connector on the cord. (You need not worry about connecting the cord to the wrong connector, as there will only be one matching connector on any Android tablet.) Plug the wall adapter into an electrical socket, and on most tablets, the screen will light up with an icon of a battery and a charging indicator clearly visible on the screen.

Android Tablet Activation

 Activate your Android tablet

Before you can use your new Android tablet, you'll need to activate the tablet. This step is simpler if you already have a Google (Gmail) account, so if you don't already have one, I suggest you go to www.gmail.com and setup a free Gmail account before proceeding.

Once you've done this, you can press the power button located along the edge of the tablet to turn it on. Unlock your Android tablet by swiping (tapping and dragging) the lock icon you see on one side across the screen, or by dragging the unlocked button past a larger outer ring. (The method that works for your tablet will depend on the model of tablet, but these are the most common methods.) The tablet will ask you to choose a default language, and it will then step you through a series of questions that include choosing your Wi-Fi connection, entering its password, and entering your Gmail account's e-mail address and password. Answer all the questions as prompted, and in a short time, your Android tablet will be ready for use.

Controls and Layout of the Android tablets

Take the time to get familiar with your Android tablet. If your Android tablet is fresh out of the box, you should take the time to get familiar with your new tablet; doing so from a hardware perspective will pay off in the long run. The device's slim yet solid design is mostly occupied by the sharp, high resolution display.

The exact layout of your tablet will vary, but all Android tablets contain certain items at various locations, such as a power off/on switch, volume buttons, and a connector used to charge the device and to transfer files (such as photos) to a computer. The following illustration shows the location of controls and connectors on a typical Android tablet. If you have not done so, you should take the time to become familiar with the controls and connectors for your Android tablet.

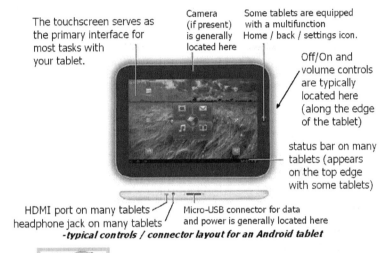

The touchscreen serves as the primary interface for most tasks with your tablet.

Camera (if present) is generally located here

Some tablets are equipped with a multifunction Home / back / settings icon.

Off/On and volume controls are typically located here (along the edge of the tablet)

status bar on many tablets (appears on the top edge with some tablets)

HDMI port on many tablets
headphone jack on many tablets

Micro-USB connector for data and power is generally located here

-typical controls / connector layout for an Android tablet

Having problems??? When in doubt, reboot. Your Android tablet is a sophisticated computer, and like all computers, it may hiccup for unexplainable reasons at times. If your tablet freezes or locks up and refuses to respond to any actions, perform a hard reset. (You needn't worry about losing any memory settings with this type of reset; it just halts any programs currently running and shuts down your device.) Hold the power button depressed for at least 30 seconds, until you see a menu appear, typically with three options: Power Off, Airplane Mode, or Restart. Tap Restart, then tap OK at the next prompt, and your Android tablet will restart.

If you are experiencing an unusually high number of system lock-ups, make sure your battery charge level is not very low. A nearly fully-drained battery is a common cause of random freezes with your tablet (or with any Android-based device).

What's an Android?

(Fair warning: reading the following is NOT likely to aid in the use of your tablet, This is strictly a nice to know topic, which is why I tacked this onto the end of this chapter.)

You may be aware of the fact that your tablet is an Android tablet. But in case this is all you know about Android, here's the trivia for you. All computers have operating systems, which are sets of software instructions that act as a traffic cop of sorts, performing basic functions behind the scenes: how the screen gets displayed, how sounds are played, what happens when you press a key, and so on. The operating system used by your tablet is named Android; other popular small computer operating systems include Microsoft Windows and Apple's iOS. Android was developed by Google, and it was developed to

serve as an operating system for mobile devices, which explains why Android powers a large chunk of the worlds' smartphones. The cute little robot that you see often is the official symbol of the Android operating system. (Android's parentage also explains why so many Google products, such as the Chrome web browser, Google PlayStore, and your entire contacts list under gMail are so seamlessly integrated into the interface of your Android tablet.).

12

*Another interesting tidbit is that various versions of Android have been named after tasty treats, beginning with the very first release version. If you tap your **Settings** icon and choose **System** > **About**, you'll see the version number of Android used by your tablet. Each version provides assorted new features and improvements. At the time of this writing, the versions are:*

Android 4.4	KitKat
Android 4.1-4.3	Jelly Bean
Android 4.0	Ice Cream Sandwich
Android 3.X	Honeycomb
Android 2.3	Gingerbread
Android 2.2	FroYo (short for frozen yogurt)
Android 2.0-2.1	Éclair
Android 1.6	Donut
Android 1.5	Cupcake

The new version releases that are more recent include the following improvements:

Gingerbread	Redesigned Home page; speed improvements; support for front-facing cameras.
Honeycomb	The first Android update geared specifically at tablets provided many tablet features, including a system bar, an action bar, redesigned keyboard for easier typing on larger screens, and a 2-pane

	email user interface.
Ice cream sandwich	Revised user interface, easier-to-create folders, improved camera app with time lag, panorama, and zoom while filming abilities, redesigned "People" app with social networking integration.
Jelly bean	Major user interface redesign, user-installable keyboard maps, improved voice search, multichannel audio, Bluetooth low energy and A/V profile support; improved game graphics, redesigned camera interface, numerous security improvements.
KitKat	Redesigned interface, wireless printing support, web views based on Chromium engine, settings access no longer uses multi-pane view.
Key Lime Pie (under development as of this writing)	The next major release of the Android O/S is still under development as this book goes to electronic 'press.' It is rumored to have a unified chat system and greatly expanded music support.

If your tablet is running a version of Android older than 'Ice Cream Sandwich,' it may be worth your while to check at the website for the manufacturer of your tablet to see if there is an update available. The update process varies from model to model of tablet, but it may be as simple as choosing an 'update' option from your settings screen.

Finally, while Google developed the Android operating system, they did not build the software entirely from scratch. Android is based on Linux, a minicomputer operating system that traces its roots back decades, to research at Bell labs (which back then was part of the one and only phone company in the United States.) Because Android is based on Linux, it is much more stable than that other popular small computer operating system (not naming names here, but it begins with a "W"...)

Chapter 2: User-Interface Tips, Tricks, and Traps

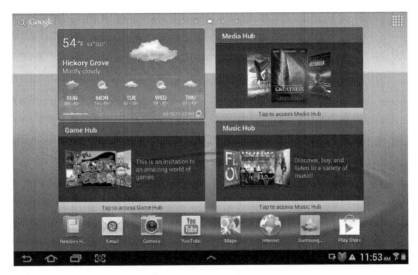

The **user interface** (that's techno-speak for "the way you get along with the device") is fairly intuitive on an Android tablet, if you've used a touchscreen device before (such as most modern cellphones). On the other hand, if your Android tablet is your first touchscreen device, you'll definitely want to get an idea of how you use various actions, by tapping or sliding one or more fingers along the screen in different ways. And through the use of the user interface, there are things that you can do to make the way that you use your tablet more efficient, and that is what this chapter is all about.

Know how to come home. One of the first things any young child learns is how to come home, and any new tablet user should know how to get to the home screen as well. Your Android tablet has a home screen- and depending on the version of the Android operating system, you may have multiple home screens, each of which can be customized to your liking. On most tablets, you can get to the home screens from anywhere, by tapping the Home icon at the edge of the screen (the icon is shaped like an up-arrow or an outline of a house, depending on your point of view, and looks like this):

Once you are at any of your home screens, you can navigate using one or two fingers (and it doesn't matter which fingers are used). If the Android tablet is your first touch screen device, you should be familiar with a number of different finger actions that you can perform, which brings us to the next tip:

Know the finger actions used by your Android tablet. On all Android-based tablets, there are six different finger movements that you can perform. These include the tap, the swipe, the double tap, the long press, the spread, and the pinch.

The tap is the most commonly-used finger action, and it refers to a single tap of an object on your screen. The tap is the equivalent of a mouse click on a traditional computer, and you can use it to launch an app (with a tap of its icon), select a menu option, or fill in a choice in a dialog box.

The swipe refers to a left or right motion using one finger. You place the finger at one side of the screen, and while holding your finger on the screen, swipe left or right to the other side. On most tablets, you can move between home screens by swiping left or right.

The double tap is the equivalent of a double click of a mouse on a traditional computer, and it simply refers to a fast tap twice on a given object or icon. In many apps, a double tap will zoom in (or out) within an image.

The long press refers to pressing and holding your finger on a specific item, icon, or part of the screen until a menu or a list of options appears. (You may occasionally see the long press referred to as a tap-and-hold operation.)

The pinch takes two fingers: you touch both fingers on the screen while they are spread apart, and while holding the fingers on the screen, you bring them together. This action is commonly used to zoom out on maps, or to shrink the size of an image.

The spread is the exact opposite of the pinch, starting with both fingers placed against the screen while holding them together, and spreading both fingers apart while keeping the fingers on the screen. This action is commonly used to zoom in on maps, or to enlarge the size of an image.

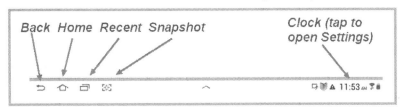 **Know the purpose of the various buttons at the bottom of your tablet.** There are a number of buttons, or *icons,* that are visible, primarily within the Navigation Bar at the bottom of any home screen, and at times in various other areas. It's helpful to know what actions these buttons perform, so here's a helpful rundown on the buttons you'll commonly see on most Android tablets: (Depending on your model and version of the Android operating system you may see other buttons, but these are the most common.) The following illustration shows the icons on a Samsung Galaxy Tab.

Back Home Recent Snapshot   Clock (tap to open Settings)

And the illustration that follows shows the icons as they appear on Google's Nexus 7 tablet.

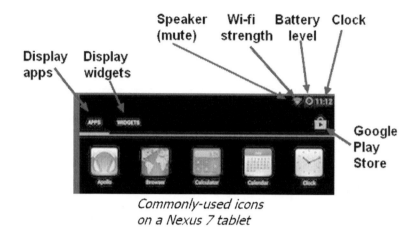

Commonly-used icons
on a Nexus 7 tablet

And as promised, here is a rundown of exactly what functions are performed by the various buttons on your screen.

Q	Search: Use this button to search your Android tablet for files, or to search the internet.
☐▪▪	Apps: This button displays a screen showing all of your apps. If you have more apps than will fit on a single screen, you can swipe to the left to reveal additional screens with your remaining apps.
●	Dictation: Use this button to dictate to your Android tablet. (Applies to tablets running Android 'jelly bean' version 4.2.2 or higher)
◁	Back: Use this button to go back to a prior action.
△	Home: This button returns you to the Home screen.
⧉	Recent: This button displays a menu of recently-opened apps or files.

☼	Settings: Use this button to display a menu with various settings that determine the behavior of your Android tablet.
✕	Close: Visible within most apps, the Close button is used to close an app or close a window.
⋖	Share: Use the Share button to share files or data stored on your tablet with others. You can share by means of e-mail, or with social media such as Facebook.
▦	Snapshot: On tablets equipped with a snapshot button, you can tap this button to capture a graphic image of the entire screen. The image is saved to the Pictures\Screenshots folder of your tablet, and Chapter 7 explains how you can access these files.

Adjusting your tablet's settings

Know how to get to all of the settings on your tablet. There are a number of settings that control various aspects of your tablet, and these can all be reached from the Settings screen. To get there, on most tablets you can press and drag down from the top edge of the screen to reveal a quick settings menu. On other tablets, you can tap the clock in the Navigation Bar (at the lower right), and a quick settings menu will appear. The following illustration shows a typical example of a quick settings menu. (Most quick settings menus use a jet black background; in this image, the colors have been reversed for better readability.)

Another example of a quick settings menu in this case, from a Samsung Galaxy Tab 10.1) is shown in the following illustration.

You can use the options on this menu to adjust commonly-used settings, such as your default Wi-Fi connection, volume levels, and screen rotation. You can also touch the Settings option (the icon in the shape of a gear) within this quick settings menu to display a complete settings screen, one example of which is shown in the illustration that follows. With many models of tablets, the settings screen will be divided into two halves. Various categories of settings will appear on the left, with appropriate settings for each setting category appearing on the right, as shown here (this variety is common with 10-inch tablets).

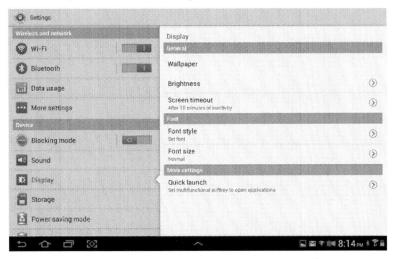

You can swipe up or down in the left half to reveal additional categories, and tap any category to reveal the settings within the right half of the screen.

On other models of Android tablets, you will see a list of overall categories of settings, and tapping any single category in the list will bring up another screen of settings that apply to that category. The following screen shows an example of this type of settings screen; this variety is common with 7-inch tablets.

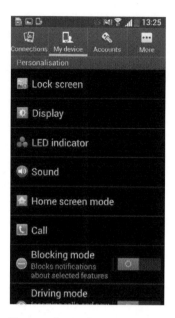

For each setting, you can tap check boxes or adjust sliders as is appropriate for the particular setting.

Adjust your font sizes to make reading easiest on YOU. You can easily adjust the font sizes to fit your needs. Use the method described above that is appropriate to your tablet to locate the Settings icon, and then tap that icon. When the Settings screen appears, tap Display. At the next screen, you can tap Font Style to choose one of the possible fonts, or you can choose Font Size to select from a menu of font sizes, as shown here.

Font size	
Tiny	◉
Small	◉
Normal	◉
Large	◉
Huge	◉
Cancel	

Note that the Android tablet font settings will control the text display of most apps, but may not have an effect within some apps. Certain app designers use their own settings menus to change the way content within those apps is displayed.

Fast E-Mail Setup

Set up Your Email Accounts quickly with Auto-Configuration. If you're like many individuals, you probably have a number of e-mail accounts. With your Android tablet, you can stay on top of your e-mail from anywhere. A later chapter will delve into using e-mail on the Android tablet in greater detail, but for now, you may find the great auto-configuration feature of most newer tablets is all you need to get your multiple e-mail accounts up and running. There are two e-mail programs built into most Android tablets-Gmail, used for Google accounts, and Email, used for all other types of accounts including corporate email. (Note that if your tablet runs an older version of Android, the 'auto-configuration' feature may not be present, in which case you'll want to refer to the Chapter 8 topic, "Setting up Android tablet e-mail manually.") Use these steps to quickly get going with e-mail:

1. Tap the Apps icon to get to your Apps screen.

2. Tap Gmail (to set up a Google account), or tap E-mail (to set up any other type of account).

3. Enter your email address and password associated with your account, and tap Next.

4. Give your account a name and enter a name to be displayed on your outgoing messages.

5. Tap Done, and you're all set. The Auto-configuration feature will set up your e-mail account, and you'll see your messages in an e-mail window. (The auto configuration works with e-mail addresses that end in any of the following: @google.com, @hotmail.com, @mac.com, @me.com, @live.com, @yahoo.com, @yahoo.co.uk, @aim.com, @aol.com, @aol.co.uk, @android.com, @btinternet.com, @gmail.com, and @googlemail.com.)

Once your e-mail has been set up, you can get into your e-mail at any time by going to the Home screen, tapping Apps, and then tapping the Gmail or E-mail icons. (See Chapter 8 for more details on the use of e-mail.)

Keyboard Use

Become familiar with your tablet's keyboard. Most Android tablets do not have a built-in physical keyboard. Instead, when textual input is required, a soft keyboard appears on the lower half of the screen, similar to the following illustration (your model may differ somewhat in appearance).

All Android tablet keyboards are *adaptive*, meaning that some keys will change purpose, depending on what you are doing at that point in time. The Enter key, for example, has different modes on an Android tablet. On most tablets, these modes are:

Enter: In this mode, the key serves the purpose of the traditional Enter or Return key on a conventional keyboard. Tapping the Enter key causes a new line to appear within your text.

Go: This variation of the key is typically used when web surfing, or to indicate the completion of an action within an app.

Search: The search key appears when you are performing some type of a search on your tablet.

Next: This variation of the key appears when you are entering information into fields of a form. You use the Next key to move from one field to the next.

Done: This variation of the key appears when you are entering information into the last field of a multi-field form.

Another multipurpose key generally appears to the immediate right of the spacebar. Hold this key down, and a menu appears that lets you enter any of the following characters: the ampersand, apostrophe, exclamation point, question mark, or comma.

Finally, on the bottom row to the left or right of the spacebar, you will generally see a 'SYM' or symbols key. Pressing this key shifts the keyboard into symbols mode, allowing you to type many of the special characters that you see above the numeral keys on a conventional keyboard. These include:

$$+ \; \_ \; \times \div = \% \; \pounds \; \text{€} \; \yen \; \text{₩} \; @ \; \# \; \$ \; / \; ^ \; \& \; * \; (\;) \; - \; ' \; '' \; : \; ;$$
$$! \; ? \; , \; .$$

Many of these admittedly odd key placements are the result of design compromises necessary to accommodate a full set of keys in a limited amount of space. An Android tablet is not the ideal device to attempt a great deal of touch typing on, but if you must perform a large amount of typing, there are alternatives. You can purchase a Bluetooth keyboard to use with most Android tablets (but before making such a purchase, check your tablet's online 'help' screens to see if your model supports the Bluetooth standard). Portable Bluetooth keyboards can commonly be found at aftermarket electronics retailers such as Best Buy and Radio Shack, and typically retail for under $50.00 US.

Make the keyboard larger. Most Android tablet apps work in portrait or landscape mode, and the keyboard is much larger and easier to use in landscape mode. You can rotate most Android tablets 90 degrees to get a landscape view of the keyboard, for an easier typing experience.

When typing large amounts of text, try the use of the voice dictation feature of many Android tablets. Heavy duty word processing on an Android tablet (or any similarly sized tablet) is going to be somewhat challenging due to the combination of a soft keyboard and a screen size that is smaller than that of a traditional laptop or desktop computer. One time saving tip when doing a lot of typing on many newer Android tablets is to try using the voice dictation feature. Any time the keyboard is visible, tap the microphone key to the left of the spacebar. (If there is no microphone symbol on your keyboard, your model of tablet does not support this feature.) After tapping the microphone key you can then dictate text, and the text will appear within whatever app you are using. At the same time, the "Tap to speak" phrase changes to read "Tap to pause," and you can tap this area to alternate between performing dictation and a 'standby' mode (where spoken words are ignored). While you are in voice dictation mode, a small icon of a keyboard also appears. You can tap this icon to drop out of voice dictation mode and return to using the soft keyboard.

Your tablet really does have a Caps Lock key. For those times when you need to type a string of characters as ALL UPPERCASE LETTERS, the Android tablet does have the equivalent of a PC's Caps Lock key. Just double-tap the Shift key and both Shift keys will turn a different color shade or appear with a small underline on the keys, indicating that you are in Caps Lock mode. Type your upper case letters, then press the Shift key once more to drop out of Caps Lock mode.

Use the period shortcut for some commonly used punctuation characters. On many newer tablets, you can hold down the period key until a menu of punctuation characters appears, then tap the desired character to enter that character.

Your finger can serve as an insertion pointer. When editing large amounts of text, tap your finger on any empty area to display an Editing Tool. You can then press on the Editing tool and move your fingertip within the text that you already typed, then release and edit the text as desired. When done editing, tap again at the end of the text, and continue typing.

Access the Cut-Copy-and-Paste options with a long-press on any word. If you need to cut or copy and paste during text editing, long-press on any single word, and within most text editing apps (including the built-in Memo app), cut / copy / paste editing options will appear, along with two selection handles. Drag the selection handles to highlight the desired text, then long-press on the desired text, and choose Cut or Copy. To paste the cut or copied text elsewhere, just tap at the desired location, and tap Paste.

Chapter 3: Android tablet Apps Tips, Tricks and Traps

In this chapter, we look at the power of apps to add significant features and capabilities to your Android tablet. Your tablet would be impressive if it were only used for viewing digital content such as books and magazines, for checking e-mail and social media, for watching movies and TV shows, and for web browsing. But with a range of apps available from the Google PlayStore and other sources, you can transform your Android tablet in an unlimited number of ways. Using apps, you can literally transform your tablet into a news or weather information center, an e-book reader, a sports scoreboard, an international language translator, a customized radio station, a medical adviser, or a personal butler that reminds you of every appointment on your busy daily schedule. And of course, you can use an app to make your Android tablet into a game platform, so that you can play a few rounds of Angry Birds. This chapter will first detail various tips, tricks, and traps for apps in general, in a section we like to call 'Apps 101.' We will follow that with a listing of ten apps that we feel that no Android tablet should be without.

Apps 101

The real power of an Android tablet comes in the form of apps, and you'll need to know how to get to your apps, add new apps, and arrange your most-often used apps on your home screen.

About your Home Screens and your Apps Screens

When you first power up your tablet and unlock the screen by swiping the lock icon to one side, by default you will be at your home screen. The following illustration shows an example of a home screen. These not only differ from model to model of tablet, they can also be heavily customized to fit your liking, and this chapter will explain how you can do this.

A typical Android tablet home screen (yours will differ)

In addition to the home screens, the screens that you'll probably use most often are the apps screens, and like the home screens, there can be more than one, depending on the number of apps you've installed on your tablet. You get to the apps screens by touching the Apps icon, which resembles a collection of tiny squares (often enclosed within a circle), as shown here:

And the following illustration (taken from the screen of a Google Nexus 7 tablet) shows just one example of an apps screen, although yours is certain to differ, because the actual appearance of your apps screen depends on what apps you've installed.

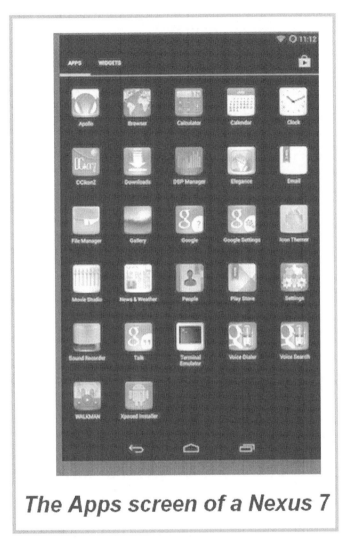

The Apps screen of a Nexus 7

The following illustration shows an apps screen from another popular model of tablet; this particular example is that of a Samsung Galaxy Tab 10.1.

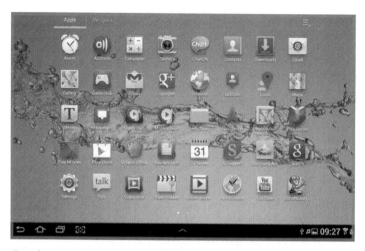

On the apps screen, you'll notice that at the upper left on most tablets, there are two icons that you can tap labeled Apps and Widgets. In a nutshell, here's the difference between the two: apps, short for applications, are mini-programs that run on your tablet to perform whatever task that you might like to perform. You may open an app to check your e-mail, view your calendar, play movies or a YouTube video, or read a book. Apps have the power to add significant features and functionality to your tablet, as tips in this chapter demonstrate.

Widgets are also apps, but they are apps of a special type. Widgets are apps that are displayed on the screen in the background, even when the screen contains other information underneath. Some built-in widgets that are supplied with most Android tablets include an analog clock, a current temperature app supplied by The Weather Channel, and a calendar.

Know how to add to, remove, and rearrange your home screen pages. As you add items to your home screen, on most tablets additional home screens will be added automatically as room is needed for your newly-added items. You'll probably want to add commonly-used apps

34

or widgets to your home screens. You can easily do so, using the following steps:

1. Tap Home to get to the Home screen where you want to place the app (or widget).

2. Tap the Apps icon.

3. Swipe to one side, if needed, to move between apps pages and find the desired app (or widget).

4. Perform a long press (press and hold the app or widget) until the Home screen appears, slide it to the desired location, and lift your finger.

You can move an app or widget icon to another location on a home screen using these steps:

1. Tap and hold the icon.

2. Slide your finger to the desired location. (You can move an existing icon out of the way, by slowly sliding into the existing icon, and you can move the app between home screens, by sliding the app toward the edge of the screen.

3. Lift your finger. When you do so, the icon drops into its new position.

You can also add folders to your home screens to better organize items on your tablet; for example, if you've collected a large number of vacation photographs, you might have these stored in different folders.)

Installing Apps

Apps for your Android tablet (or for any tablet computer, for that matter) are actually computer programs, engineered to handle a specific task. As such, they must be installed on your Android tablet, which is a sophisticated computer in its own right. You install apps on your Android tablet by first locating the app from an app source such as the

Google PlayStore. You then install the app on your Android tablet by tapping the 'Install' button that appears at the upper right for the page of any given app. After the app has been installed on your Android tablet, you can tap the app to launch it. Once the app exists on your tablet, you can get to it at any time, by tapping the Apps icon on the Home screen, and locating and tapping on the icon for the particular app.

 **Find and install the app you want.** Tap the Apps icon on your Home screen, and locate and tap the Google PlayStore icon on the next page that appears (the icon looks like this):

When you open the PlayStore for the first time, you'll need to read the terms of service and touch Accept to continue. After doing so, sign in to your Google account (or create a new Google account if you prefer).

Next, navigate to the desired app. (You can also search for an app by typing the name of the app or a search term, such as "maps" or "angry birds" in the search box. You can also browse among the categories that appear at the top of the Google PlayStore by tapping a category name, and then tapping a category at the left. The Google PlayStore has thousands of apps divided into several categories that include games, books and reference, business, comics, communication, education, entertainment, health, lifestyle, media, medical, music, news, productivity, shopping, social, travel, weather, and more.) The following illustration shows just one example of various available apps within the Google PlayStore.

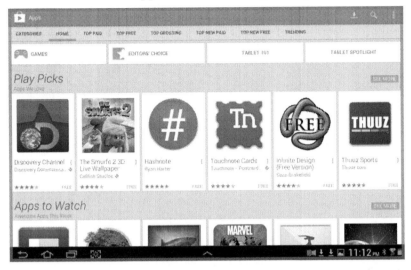

Tap any app within the PlayStore and you will be taken to the main page for that particular app. When you find an app that you want to download, tap Install. When the download completes, the app's icon will appear on your Apps screen, and you can tap the icon to open and use the app.

Uninstalling Apps

There may be times you'll want to remove an app, perhaps because it's not what you expected, or it is a game you've outgrown, or something better comes along. You can remove an app from your tablet by going to the 'Uninstall' screen within your Apps screen. Use the following steps to remove an unwanted app:

1. Tap the Home icon (the icon in the shape of a house) to get to your Home screen.

2. At the Home screen, tap the Apps icon (the icon shaped like a group of tiny squares), as shown in the illustration.

3. When the Apps screen appears, tap the Menu icon (on most Android tablets, this icon appears as three horizontal bars, as shown in the next illustration).

When the menu opens as shown, tap 'Uninstall.'

Tap Menu icon at upper right, then choose 'Uninstall' from menu that appears.

4. A new Apps window with the title "Uninstall" at the top of the screen will appear, and you can tap the app that you want to uninstall. You will be asked for confirmation of the removal, and once you click OK, the app will be uninstalled.

Note that the app may still appear in your Downloads list even after you have uninstalled the app. This simply means that you downloaded the app at some point in time, even when it isn't installed. Also, if you pay for an app, install it, and uninstall it shortly thereafter (perhaps because the app did not perform as expected), in most cases you won't be charged for the app. Exactly how long is "shortly after" depends on the policies of the app developer, and these vary.)

Also note that if you are trying to delete apps because you are concerned that valuable storage space is being wasted by unused apps, you are probably wasting your time in trying to reclaim space by deleting apps. It is true that apps consume storage space, but in the grand scheme of things, the space consumed by an app is relatively tiny in comparison to the space consumed by your photographs, music files, and especially those vacation videos you've downloaded from your camcorder. If storage space is truly an issue and if your tablet is equipped with a micro SD RAM card expansion slot, your time would be much better spent installing a micro SD RAM card in the expansion slot of your tablet. You could then store your files on the card. (Chapter 7 provides details on how you can do this.)

Note that deleting an app also wipes away any subscription information you may have saved in the app, so you should do this only if you are certain that you do not want to use the app in the future.

Keep in mind that there are some apps that cannot be uninstalled, as they are part of the Android operating system on your Android tablet. For example, you cannot remove the Google PlayStore app. (Given that Google designed the operating system, it's understandable that the company would not be terribly excited at the thought of your removing the PlayStore app.)

Troubleshooting Apps

As mentioned earlier, apps are computer programs. And like all computer programs, they will at times fail to operate as promised, misbehave, or go absolutely haywire. When an app fails to operate as expected, your steps in resolving the issue will vary greatly depending on what type of behavior the app exhibited in the first place. Some app failures fall into the 'hiccup' category, in which case it may be best to chalk it up to the "evil gods of operating systems" and to move on in life. Other failures can go beyond the level of major annoyance, causing your Android tablet to completely lock up or otherwise become unresponsive. If an app misbehaves, crashes, or completely locks up your Android tablet, here are some procedures that you can try, ranging in ascending order from minor (meaning, 'let's hope this works') to major (meaning, 'let's hope you don't have to resort to this')-

1. Close and restart the app. Without subjecting you to a heavy dose of techno-babble, let's just say that Android-based computers tend to be more stable than some small computer operating systems (Windows, not that anyone is pointing fingers) because each Android app runs in something called protected space. From a programming point of view, each app can "play inside its own sandbox." This means that in theory, the abnormal operation of an app should not affect the entire operating system, nor should it have an effect on other apps. When an app misbehaves, the least troublesome step is to completely close the app, and then restart the app. If this does not fix the problem you can move on to-

2. "Reboot" your Android tablet by turning it off and back on. Shut off your tablet. Wait 10 seconds, and power the Android tablet back on, then try the app again. If the restart fails to bring your machine back to normal operation, you can resort to-

3. Perform a soft reset on your Android tablet. With the tablet powered up, press and hold the power button depressed until you see a "Tablet options" menu appear on the

screen with options that generally include: Power Off, Airplane mode, and Restart. Tap 'Restart' and confirm this choice by tapping "OK" in the next dialog box, and your Android tablet will shut down and restart. You may notice a distinct difference in the appearance of the startup sequence this time, as your Android tablet will take somewhat longer to start up than it normally does. Hopefully, this will fix the issue, because the most drastic step will also result in a definite loss of settings. But if you must resort to the most drastic step--

4. Perform a hard reset (reset your Android tablet to its default directory settings). **Be warned that if you use this last resort, you will need to reset your username and e-mail account information that you've registered in the device with Google, and you will have to reinstall all of your apps (and reenter any user settings that may have been stored in these apps).** To perform this ultimate reboot, if you can get to the operating system, use the menus applicable to your tablet to get to the Settings screen. Locate and tap the Back Up / Reset option, and then tap Factory Data Reset.

If you can't get to the operating system, try the following steps, which will work with most Android tablets:

1. With the tablet turned off, simultaneously press and hold the Volume Up and Power buttons.

2. Release the Power button when a manufacturer logo appears, but continue to hold the Volume Up button until a recovery menu appears.

3. Use the Volume buttons to navigate the menu and select wipe data / factory reset.

4. Press Home to choose the selection.

5. Press the Volume Up button to confirm your choice, and your tablet should begin the hard reset process.

If your tablet still has operational issues after this type of reset, it is definitely time to get on the phone with the customer service department for your particular tablet. (If you've misplaced the documentation, you can typically find contact information by performing a Google search on the manufacturer and model name, followed by the words 'contact customer service.'

Ten FREE Apps No Android tablet Should Be Without

As promised, here's a listing of ten FREE apps (you heard correctly, the price is zero, nada, zilch) that the author believes should be on the Apps page of every Android tablet. This is an admittedly subjective list, but each of these apps has also received an above-average to excellent rating (between 4 and 5 stars) from reviewers. To find and download any of these free apps, simply search the Google PlayStore for any of the titles named on the following pages.

Crackle

Crackle is an outstanding source of FREE movies and TV shows (that's correct, as in 'no subscriber or pay-per-view fees involved). With the Crackle app installed on your Android tablet, you get immediate access to thousands of full-length Hollywood movies and TV shows. At the time this was written, the lineup on Crackle included movies like Pineapple Express, Big Daddy, Joe Dirt, Mr. Deeds, Alien Hunter, The Deep, Panic Room, S.W.A.T., and hundreds of others. Also in the Crackle lineup are dozens of TV shows like Seinfeld, The Prisoner, Marvel Comics' Iron Man animated series, All in the Family, and Chosen, just to name a few. Twenty new movies and TV episodes are added to the lineup each month, from genres that include action, anime, comedy, crime, horror, thrillers, and sci-fi. Crackle is truly free internet entertainment at its best, and if entertainment is one planned use for your tablet, you should definitely have the Crackle app as one of your apps.

USA TODAY

From what multiple reviewers and this author say, the USA Today app for the Android tablet is the kind of app that every newspaper app should be. The content is beautiful, optimized to take advantage of the larger screen. Unlike many newspaper apps for Android-based tablets, the content is all free on this one; there are no subscription services to pay whatsoever. While you're online, the app feeds you constant updates, making sure you've received the latest news and information, and you can pull down stories for offline reading when you don't have Internet access.

The organization is logical, the formatting is colorful, and from a user friendliness standpoint it's a cinch to navigate. There is a wonderfully-intuitive 'swipe to the left or right' action within the main content viewer that automatically jumps you between stories in the smaller Articles window on the left, or you can tap any story within the Articles window to bring up the corresponding story on the right. Stories are laced with top-notch photography and occasionally with vivid video narratives. As an online newspaper, this implementation absolutely rocks. Oh, and did we mention that it's free? As a newspaper, USA Today on the Android tablet deserves five stars.

The Weather Channel

For the kind of in-depth weather reporting that you've come to rely on, you no longer need to turn to a cable or satellite TV channel. The Weather Channel is now no further than your Android tablet. Get animated and customizable radar maps; immediate, 36-hour, and ten day forecasts; severe weather alerts for the US and Europe; the ability to save multiple locations; and a "find me" feature that provides you with pinpoint local weather, based on your GPS location. Even the local pollen counts, which are often omitted from other sources, can be found at The Weather Channel. One particularly nice feature is the ability to touch a 'Video' button and get the local forecast for your area on demand from one of the TV anchors for The Weather Channel.

ESPN Sports Center Free

When it comes time to talk sports around the office water cooler on a Monday morning, you'll never be stumped for a score again if you install the ESPN Sports Center app on your Android tablet. You'll get scores, team standings, and news from hundreds of sports leagues worldwide. The variety of sports provided by ESPN Sports Center is just short of breathtaking- you'll find NFL and college football, NBA and college basketball, Major League Baseball, NHL Ice Hockey, and most other NCAA sports. If you are a big soccer fan, you'll find coverage of the Premier League, UEFA Champions League, the World Cup, and hundreds of additional soccer leagues and tournaments. NASCAR and Indy racing fans will find full coverage of motor sports, and golf, tennis, rugby, and cricket fans are all covered as well. If you are looking to keep up with the sports scene, you'll find it all in the ESPN Sports Center app.

Calculator Plus Free by Digitech

This app earned a listing in a "best free apps" article written by USA Today, and for good reason. Calculator Plus consistently earns five stars from reviewers, thanks to its intuitive interface, its feature set, and its ease of use. It is a simple calculator with just the basics, but those basics likely make for 98% of what most people need in a calculator. The app takes advantage of the Android tablet's large screen to present a very basic, but totally functional desktop style calculator. You get the basic keys (+), (-), (*), (/), and (%), along with a backspace key that works intuitively in concert with the calculator's multiline display, allowing you to use the backspace key to "undo" past operations. This free app is ad supported, but the ads are unobtrusive and nearly impossible to accidentally hit while using the calculator function keys.

Adobe Reader by Adobe Systems

If you spend a fair amount of time working with documents that are in the portable document format (pdf) pioneered by Adobe, you may as well opt for the Adobe Reader as an app on your Android tablet. While you can open a PDF file in the default Android viewer, the Adobe Reader offers more features in terms of working with PDF documents. You can make the print larger or smaller at the touch of the magnification button. You can navigate in more ways, viewing documents in a single page format, or as a continuous series of pages. And you can search through a searchable pdf for a phrase, or e-mail a pdf as an attachment, things that you cannot do with the Android native viewer.

iTranslate Free Translator

iTranslate is a great free app that does language translation. If you're a student of languages or you do a lot of international travel, you'll definitely want to have this one on your Android tablet. The app does a magnificent job of combining voice recognition with voice output, so you can speak and see your language. The app will translate words, phrases, and entire sentences into any one of more than 50 languages. These words of one reviewer (as posted on Amazon's apps website) do a great job of describing the functionality of the program:

"I am fluent in several languages and was pretty impressed with this app. I tested with a realistic tourist phrase which was fairly complex "I would like to visit your best art museum. Can you give me a recommendation and how to get there."

I selected English from the left drop down list, typed in the phrase in English, and selected the second language from a drop down list on the right. I was impressed with the translation, the grammar was perfectly correct. Next to the text there was a button which pronounced the translation. The pronunciation was excellent and sounded like a native speaker. The intonations sounded "computer generated" but completely understandable. I tested Russian and Spanish." The reviewer goes on to state that "this was the first random sentence that came to mind, I did not try to find a phrase that would be translated well. I was quite impressed with the results."

iTranslate will even let you e-mail a translated message, share it via Twitter, or copy it into memory for use with another app. Supported languages (at the time of this writing) include the following: Afrikaans, Albanian, Arabic, Belarusian, Bulgarian, Catalan, Chinese Simplified, Chinese Traditional, Croatian, Czech, Danish, Dutch, English, Estonian, Finnish, French, Galician, German, Greek, Hebrew, Hindi, Hungarian, Icelandic, Indonesian, Italian, Irish, Japanese, Korean, Latvian, Lithuanian, Macedonian, Malay, Maltese, Norwegian, Persian, Polish, Portuguese, Romanian, Russian, Serbian, Slovak, Slovenian, Spanish, Swahili, Swedish, Tagalog, Thai, Turkish, Ukrainian, Vietnamese, Welsh, and Yiddish.

WebMD for Android

In these recessionary times of spiraling health care costs and many underinsured due to circumstances often beyond one's control, it's great to have an app like WebMD. WebMD is the popular online medical reference library brought to app form on the Android tablet. Using the symptom checker feature, you can choose the body part that is troubling you, select your symptoms, and learn about potential conditions or issues. WebMD's exhaustive drugs and treatments database gives you information on drugs, supplements, and vitamins. A First Aid Essentials guide to medical emergencies is available offline, so whether you have a wi-fi connection or not, you'll still be able to access the treatment essentials outlined in the First Aid Essentials guide.

Dolphin Browser

The built-in web browser that comes as a part of the Android tablet implementation of Google's Android operating system works well enough, but there are superior web browsers, and the Dolphin Browser definitely falls in the "superior" class. You get a true desktop browsing experience with the Dolphin browser, it supports add-ons, and handles bookmarks with far more flexibility than the default browser built into the Android tablet. Considering the price—free—you can't go wrong with the addition of this app.

Facebook

Anyone who hasn't crawled out from under a rock for the past decade is familiar with what Facebook is about. So, why do you need this app, when you could just go to facebook.com in your web browser? The answer, in a nutshell, is interactivity with other apps on your Android tablet. You can share photos, e-mail, and other digital content directly between compatible apps (like Google's Gmail, Twitter, and Skype). And the app is smooth and responsive, making for a better experience than just logging into Facebook with a web browser.

Chapter 4: Free Books, Movies, and Music Tips, Tricks and Traps

Your Android tablet is a great source of information and entertainment, but let's face it: content costs, and quality contents costs more. Like everyone else, authors and songwriters certainly expect to eat (no surprise there), and production costs skyrocket when you get into the league of big-name entertainers and the costs of producing those Hollywood blockbusters that you're fond of watching on the 'small screen'. But there are great sources of free, quality content available for your Android tablet. My favorite source is one that in a way, you've likely already paid for (and continue paying for) over the years: I'm speaking of your tax-supported, local public library.

Borrow content for free from your public library. Many Android tablet owners are oblivious to the fact that most public libraries now loan books, movies, music, and other digital content for Android-based tablets (as well as for other digital products like smartphones, Apple iPads, and Amazon Kindles.) In the United States alone, at the time of this writing, nearly 20,000 public libraries are members of a system called OverDrive Media. OverDrive Media provides an app for your Android tablet that lets you borrow content electronically from your public library. All you'll need is the app (a free download from the Google PlayStore) and your library card number. Check with your local library to see if they are a member of the OverDrive program. You should be able to check without getting out of your easy chair; do a Google search for your town's public library web site, and once you find it, look for a link that says "download e-books" or something similar. If your city does not have a membership in such a program, there are libraries that allow nonresidents to obtain a library card for an annual fee. Two, at the time of this writing, are those of Fairfax County, Virginia (www.fairfaxcounty.gov/library for more information) and the City of Philadelphia (www.freelibrary.org for more information).

Once you've found that your library is a member of the OverDrive Media service, go to the Google PlayStore, search on the term 'overdrive media console', and download the app to your Android tablet. Launch the app, and tap the "Get Books" icon at the top of the screen. At the next screen that appears, tap the "Add Library" icon at the top of the screen.

At the next screen that appears, you'll be asked for a City name or ZIP code; enter your zip code, and you'll see your local library's name in a list. Select your library by name, tap "Audiobook" or "E-book" when asked, and you'll be taken to a page for your local library, where you can borrow books, movies, and other digital content. Browse among what your library has available for lending, click on a title, and you'll see a "Borrow from library" button. Click that button, and you will be asked to enter your library card number. Enter your information, and you'll see options to download the book in e-PUB format, or to read the book in your Android tablet's web browser. (To prevent piracy of e-books, most libraries will require you to register for an Adobe Digital ID account; the registration is free.)

Different libraries have different lending policies, so you'll want to check with your local library to determine the exact length of your loan. In my resident town of Charlotte, North Carolina, books have a two-week loan with one possible renewal, and movies are good for ten days. Many libraries now offer regularly scheduled classes or workshops that teach library patrons how to download digital content, so you may want to visit your local library and sign up for such a class in your home town.

Another great way to find free books is to search for... free books! As part of regular ongoing promotions, various authors, publishers, or distributors will place their books, magazines, and occasionally, video content on sale for nothing for promotional reasons. You can take advantage of this fact by simply searching within the Google PlayStore for any desired genre of books, magazines, movies, or television and entering "0.00" as your search criteria in the Search box What appears will be items that have a price of zero dollars, zero cents on that particular day. This list will change wildly on a daily basis, so you may find it worth your while to perform this sort of a search on a regular basis.

Download free books from the Internet, and transfer these to your Android tablet using your USB cable. The final source of free books that this chapter will detail is that of the Internet itself. You can find countless sources of free e-books on the Internet. These come in a variety of file formats, and your Android tablet will also read books in Adobe Acrobat (.PDF) format, as well as files in the popular E-PUB format. Some books that you find on the web will be in the Amazon Kindle (.KZW) file format, and these cannot be read by an Android tablet. The solution for this is not overwhelmingly complex; you can download free e-book converter programs that will convert e-books from Amazon's Kindle (.KZW) format into the EPUB format readable by any Android tablet. An excellent program is called Calibre (go to www.calibre-ebook.com for details). Calibre can convert files from many formats, including the Amazon Kindle file format, into the E-PUB format. Once you convert the file, use the file transfer techniques described in Chapter 7 of this book, to transfer the e-books that you've converted to your Android tablet.

As for sources, performing a Google search for "free e-books" will return an avalanche of sites. Here is a small list to get you started:

Project Gutenberg- www.gutenberg.org

ManyBooks.net- http://manybooks.net

Google Books- http://books.google.com/

MobiPocket Free Books-www.mobipocket.com/freebooks/

An exhaustive source of free computer-based books can be found at http://freecomputerbooks.com. Finally, you'll find a surprisingly comprehensive list of textbooks that can be legally shared, at http://textbookrevolution.org. These are in .PDF format.

Chapter 5: Web Browser Tips, Tricks, and Traps

Your Android tablet has a web browser built in, which does an admirable job of letting you surf the web (but see the important note that follows, to determine whether you should be reading this chapter or the one that follows). The browser is a multi window browser that uses the tabbed interface design commonly used by many modern web browsers.

IMPORTANT NOTE: Most Android tablets offer one of two possible web browsers, and some tablets offer both. Before proceeding, you'll want to determine which browser is used by your particular tablet, as this chapter covers the first commonly-used browser, and the following chapter covers the second commonly-used browser. The first, which we will call simply the Internet browser, appears on your desktop as an icon in the shape of a world globe, and is simply labeled 'Internet.' (The following illustration shows the icon for the Internet browser.)

This browser is a scaled-down web browser based upon Google's Chrome browser technology. If this is the web browser that is on your Android tablet, you should be reading this chapter to learn about its use.

By comparison, many Android tablets come with a full implementation of Google's Chrome web browser. If your Android tablet comes with Google's Chrome web browser, you will be able to locate an icon resembling the following illustration somewhere on your apps screen:

If your Android tablet uses the Google Chrome browser, you should skip ahead to the following chapter, which details the use of the Chrome browser. If your tablet offers both browsers, as some do, you can take your pick, and revert to the chapter that details the browser you've chosen. (If your model of Android tablet does offer the use of either browser, the author highly recommends that you go with the Chrome browser for your web browsing, as it offers significantly more features than the scaled down Internet browser described in this chapter.)

Using the Web Browser

To get to the browser, get to the Home screen and tap the Internet icon, OR tap your Apps icon, then locate and tap the Internet icon, as shown here.

The browser will open, as shown in the following illustration.

To navigate to a particular website, just tap the URL (web address) field that appears at the top of the browser. When you do this, the keyboard will appear, and you can type the URL of the desired web site and tap the Go button at the bottom right of the keyboard to navigate to the site.

You can use the following navigational tips when using the built-in web browser:

You can reload a web page at any time by tapping the Refresh icon (the circular arrow, as shown in the illustration).

To go back to a previous location, touch to the left arrow ("Back") icon at the upper-left corner of the screen, and the page that you previously visited will appear.

You can open a new tab to a different web site at any time by tapping the rightmost tab (it contains a '+' symbol). The URL (web address) field will appear blank in the new tab, and you can enter another web site address or search term and press the "Go" key on the keyboard.

To navigate between tabs when multiple tabs are open, simply tap the tab of any desired site to switch to that website.

Searching the Web

You can enter a search term directly into the address field of the browser. In addition to entering the URL or web site address into the browser, you can enter a search term in the URL field. Whenever the browser sees a term entered that is **not** a properly-formatted web site address, it assumes that a search phrase was entered, and passes the phrase onto Google's web search engine.

Speed up your searches with the Android tablet's dictation feature. If you need to search the web, you don't necessarily need to resort to typing in a search phrase. If your tablet supports voice recognition, you can often speak the phrase, and while the Android operating system's voice recognition isn't perfect, there's a surprisingly high chance that your tablet will correctly interpret what you said. Open a browser tab, tap in the URL field, and when the keyboard appears, tap the Microphone key that is on the lower left row of the keyboard. The keyboard will vanish, and a "Tap to pause" button will appear. Speak your search phrase slowly and clearly, then tap the "Tap to pause" button. If you're satisfied with the term that appears in the URL /search field, you can tap the Keyboard icon and then tap Go to perform the web search, or you can use the keyboard to edit the phrase as needed.

Changing your Browser Settings

Use the various options of the browser menu to make better use of the web browser. The Menu icon lists a number of useful options for the Android tablet browser. The following illustration shows the menu choices that appear when you open the browser menu. (This particular illustration is based on a Samsung Galaxy Tab; your browser menu may differ slightly in appearance, but will have similar options.

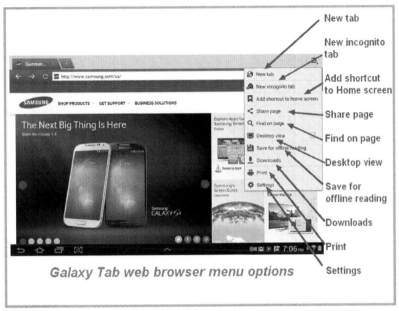

Galaxy Tab web browser menu options

If you select the Settings choice, a Settings screen appears with various settings used by the browser, as shown in the following illustration. You can use these settings to change various aspects of your browser's behavior, such as the home page displayed by default and whether web forms are automatically filled in; options to accept or clear cookie data and form data; options to enable or disable location-based tracking; various accessibility options; and assorted advanced options including your choice of search engine, whether JavaScript and plug-ins are enabled, and whether pop-ups are blocked.

On most Android tablets with 7-inch screens, tapping a category of settings on the initial Settings screen displays another screen with individual categories that can be set as desired (the following illustration shows an example of this type of settings screen).

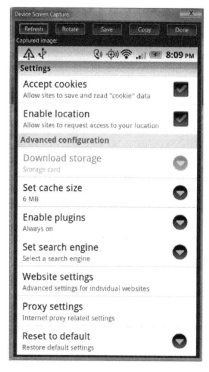

Using Bookmarks

Bookmark commonly visited pages so you can return to them quickly at a later time. As with all modern web browsers, the Android tablet browser provides the ability to bookmark sites so that you can easily return to the same site. To add a bookmark, tap the Add Bookmark icon near the upper right corner of the web browser.

A Bookmarks List will appear on your screen. In the list, tap the Add Bookmark icon. Change the name of the entry to something friendlier if you desire, and tap OK, to add the page to your bookmarked pages.

When you open a new tab, you can tap the 'Bookmarks' icon (remember, it's the one in the shape of a ribbon with a small star) to display a list of all of your bookmarked pages, then tap the desired bookmark to open that webpage.

Delete unwanted bookmarks. Tap the Bookmarks icon (the star) to go to the Bookmarks page. You can then delete any bookmark by performing a long-press on the unwanted bookmark, and choosing "Delete Bookmark" from the menu that appears.

Handy Web Browsing Tips

The "thumb and finger spread" or "thumb and finger pinch" works in the Android tablet web browser. You will often encounter web pages with text that is too small to read on the tablet's screen. Place your thumb and finger on the screen and spread them to magnify, or pinch them together to reduce the magnification.

Use "Find on this page" as a search tool. Oftentimes you will need to search a website for a particular word or phrase. To do this in the web browser, tap the Menu icon, then tap "Find on page." Enter a search term in the search field that appears, and all instances of the term will be highlighted within the text of the web page. You can use the backwards (left-arrow) and forwards (right-arrow) buttons that appear at the top right side of the web browser to move through the search results.

Let the browser complete your entry. As you begin typing characters into the search / address field, a list of suggestions appears below the field, based upon your previous entries in the browser. If you see a suggestion that matches the URL you intended to type, tap that suggestion.

Keep browser performance up through regular housecleaning. Just as browsers on your PC can be slowed over time from too many cookies or from a clogged cache, so can the Android tablet's browser. You can perform a bit of browser housecleaning on occasion with these steps:

1. Open a browser window.

2. In the upper-right corner of the browser, tap the Menu icon, and choose Settings. (This will take you to the settings page for the browser.)

3. Tap 'Privacy and Security' and at the next screen, locate and turn on the Clear History, Clear Cache, and Clear All Cookies options.

Set your browser settings to your preferences. Your tablet's web browser has a number of settings that you can use to change the operation of the browser. To get to these settings, first open a browser window. In the upper-right corner of the browser, tap the menu button and choose Settings from this window. This will take you to the settings page for the web browser. The settings are fairly self-explanatory; just keep in mind that as you select any setting, details about that setting will appear on the right (on most ten-inch tablets), and on a separate page (with most 7-inch and 8–inch tablets.

Set Home Page: By default, your browser's chosen home page appears as the starting page when you initially launch the Android tablet browser. You can change this to whatever page you want using this option. Navigate to the desired page you want to serve as your home page, tap the Set Home Page option, and tap the Use Current Page option in the menu that appears.

Privacy and Security: There are also privacy settings that affect the browsers behavior. To access the privacy settings, you will need to scroll down in the Settings screen to reveal the settings. They include Clear Cache, Clear History, Accept Cookies, Clear All Cookies Data, Remember Form Data, Clear Form Data, Enable Location and Clear Location Access, and Remember Passwords and Clear Passwords. The Clear Cache option will clear the cache, or temporary working memory of the browser, while the Clear History option clears the browser of any memory of past and visited websites.

You can set the Accept Cookies option to accept or reject 'cookies' from web sites, as desired. (Cookies are bits of information sent by web servers to your browser, and they are routinely used as a means of identifying information about a user.) The Clear All Cookies data option clears all cookies from your browser. The Remember Form Data option, when checked, tells the browser to remember information that you type into a form field for later use, and the Clear Form Data option lets you clear all saved form data on your browser's memory.

The Enable Location option lets you turn on (or off) the ability of web sites to request your location based on GPS signals, and the Passwords options let you save user names and passwords, or clear all passwords.

Accessibility: Various options within this area let you control the display of fonts within the browser, and allow you to choose inverted screen rendering (where black displays as white, and vice versa).

Advanced: Various settings in this area let you change specialized settings used by the browser. Ones covered within this chapter include Set Search Engine, Enable JavaScript, Enable Plug-Ins, Default Zoom, and Auto-Fit Pages.

Select Search Engine: This is set to Google by default, but you can change this setting to use Yahoo or Bing.

Open in background: When selected, this option causes a new window to open behind current windows.

Enable JavaScript: A large number of websites use JavaScript, a popular programming language, to display animation or other special effects. In most cases, you want to leave this option turned on, although if it causes problems with certain websites that you visit often, you may want to turn it off.

Enable plug-ins: Turn this option on to enable plug-ins that are built into websites to execute. Your choices are Always On, On Demand (in which case you will be prompted), or Off.

Open pages in overview: This forces the browser to show an overview of newly-opened pages.

Auto-Fit Pages: This option rearranges web pages automatically to fit the shape of your Android tablet.

Block Pop-Ups: By default, the browser automatically blocks pop-up windows; however, there may be instances where you need or want to see popup windows at websites. You can turn this option to on or off as desired, to block or unblock popup windows.

Bandwidth Management: Options in this area include **Preload Search Results,** which lets the browser preload high confidence search results in the background; **Page Preloading,** allowing the browser to load pages in the background, and **Load Images.** If you turn off this checkbox, web pages will be loaded with placeholders instead of actual images. The result is that most web pages that you visit will display faster. (You can always tap on the markers to display the individual images.)

 Consider an aftermarket web browser. While the default Android tablet browser does a fair job of web browsing, in the author's opinion there are better web browsers available for your tablet. You may want to consider downloading an aftermarket web browser and using it for your web browsing; there are a couple of excellent choices available that are free, and you can find them in the Google PlayStore. One is the Dolphin browser, shown in the following illustration, and the other is the Maxtor web browser.

Of the two, the author likes the Dolphin web browser, although the selection of any web browser is certainly an issue of personal choice. If you're interested, you'll find more details about the Dolphin web browser in the apps chapter of this publication.

Chapter 6: Chrome Browser Tips, Tricks, and Traps

This chapter details the use of the Google Chrome web browser. **IMPORTANT NOTE: As mentioned in the prior chapter, Android tablets are typically equipped with one of two popular web browsers, the "Internet" browser and the Google Chrome browser.**

If your web browser icon resembles the following--

--then you should be reading this chapter. If your browser icon does not resemble this icon, you should refer to the previous chapter.

While you could install other browsers on your tablet, Google Chrome is one excellent web browser, for a wealth of reasons. Back in the early days of the World Wide Web, people used web browsers just to go to internet websites. But as the Web has evolved, the uses for browsers have grown far beyond simply surfing the web. Today, a major task of web browsers is to run web-based apps. And if you ever check email within a web browser or watch a YouTube video, you are using a web-based app. One major reason for using Chrome is that it excels at the use of web-based apps- in fact, the program was designed from the ground up to run web-based apps. Another reason for using Chrome is its cross platform capabilities. Chrome runs on so many devices, including most personal computers, most smartphones, and any standard Android tablet (exceptions are the Amazon Kindle Fire and the Barnes and Noble NOOK, but neither of these are 'standard' Android tablets). The Chrome browser is also fast, it is secure, and it allows for heavy personalization. And by signing into Chrome with your Google Gmail account, you can literally take your work with you wherever you go, as long as you can get to an internet connection. Given all of these advantages, it's no surprise that most Android tablets use the Chrome browser as the default web browser.

Getting Familiar with Chrome

To launch Chrome, simply tap the Apps icon to get to your apps screen, then tap the Chrome browser icon, shown here.

When you do this, the Chrome browser opens, similar to the example shown in the illustration that follows. The illustration also shows the component parts of the Chrome browser. If this is your first look at the Chrome browser, it makes sense to get familiar with the component parts, as noted in this illustration.

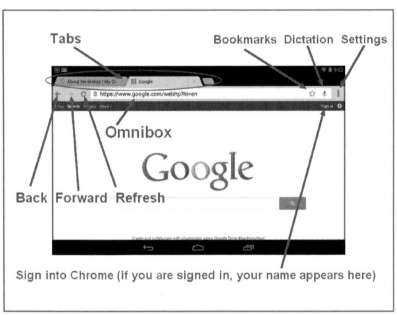

Tabs: you can navigate between multiple pages in a single Chrome window using tabs. Just click on any desired tab to show that page, or tap the new tab button to the right of the last active tab to open a new tab.

Omnibox: what some browsers refer to as the URL address bar or the web address bar is actually called the Omnibox in Chrome, because it can serve multiple purposes. Typically, you type a web address into the box and press Enter, and you are taken to that website. However, the Omnibox in Chrome is also a very powerful search tool. You can type a search phrase directly into the Omnibox, and that phrase will be passed on to the Google search engine. Within a moment, you'll see the results of your Google search.

Bookmarks button: you click the bookmarks button to save the page that you are currently viewing to your bookmarks. Bookmarks are lists of frequently visited web sites, and you can use bookmarks to quickly return to a site without having to retype the entire web address.

Navigation buttons: There are a number of navigation buttons located near the top edge of the Chrome browser, as pointed out in the illustration. These include the Back icon (takes you back to a previously visited page), the Forward icon (which takes you forward a page if you are at a previously visited page), the Refresh icon (which refreshes the contents of the Google Chrome screen), the Bookmarks button, and a Dictation button, the one shaped like a tiny microphone. (Yes, you can even dictate to your Chrome browser using any tablet that is equipped with a microphone.)

Sign in to Google Chrome. The first time that you start Google Chrome, you'll be shown a screen similar to the following example, asking if you want to sign into Chrome. (If this isn't your first time using Chrome on your tablet, you will see a link that reads "Sign into Chrome" at the upper-right corner of the browser, and you can tap this link to open a sign-in screen.)

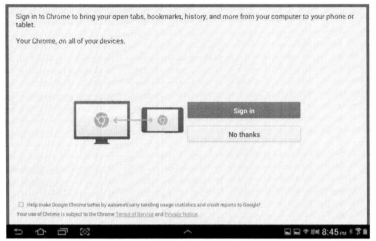

While you can click the "skip this" button to skip past this point without signing in, there are a number of advantages to signing into Chrome. One major advantage is that this enables the "take your work with you" features of Chrome. If you sign in with your Google account, you will be able to gain access to all of your bookmarks, passwords, browsing history, and Chrome settings you currently use on any computer or any mobile device that is running the Chrome browser. Signing in also enables the use of Google Drive, Google's cloud-based online storage. (See Chapter 7 for details on using Google Drive with your Android tablet.)

Like all web browsers, Chrome increases its speed and saves time by saving data from sites you've visited in the past, in a special area called history. You can get to this area by tapping the Settings icon at the upper right corner of the Chrome window, and choosing History from the menu that appears.

Basic Navigation within Chrome

To navigate to a particular website, just tap anywhere in the Omnibox that appears at the top of the browser. When you do this, the keyboard will appear, and you can type the URL of the desired web site and tap the Go button at the bottom right of the keyboard to navigate to the site.

You can use the following navigational tips when using Chrome to surf the web:

You can reload a web page at any time by tapping the Refresh icon (the circular arrow, as shown in the illustration).

To go back to a previous location, touch to the left arrow ("Back") icon at the upper-left corner of the screen, and the page that you previously visited will appear.

You can open a new tab to a different web site at any time by tapping the rightmost tab. The Omnibox will appear blank in the new tab, and you can enter another web site address or search term and press the "Go" key on the keyboard.

To navigate between tabs when multiple tabs are open, simply tap the tab of any desired site to switch to that website.

You can enter a search term directly into the Omnibox (the address field) of the browser. In addition to entering the URL or web site address into the browser, you can enter a search term in the URL field. Whenever Chrome sees a term entered that is *not* a properly-formatted web site address, it assumes that a search phrase was entered, and passes the phrase onto Google's search engine.

Speed up your searches with the Android tablet's dictation feature. If you need to search the web, you don't necessarily need to resort to typing in a search phrase; you can often speak the phrase, and while the Android operating system's voice recognition isn't perfect, there's a surprisingly high chance that it will correctly interpret what you said. Open a browser tab, tap in the Omnibox, and when the keyboard appears, tap the Microphone key that is on the lower left row of the keyboard. The keyboard will vanish, and a "Tap to pause" button will appear. (If there is no microphone key on your keyboard, your model of tablet does not support voice recognition.) Speak your search phrase slowly and clearly, then tap thc "Tap to pause" button. If you're satisfied with the term that appears in the browser, you can tap the Keyboard icon and then tap Go to perform the web search, or you can use the keyboard to edit the phrase as needed.

Changing your Chrome Browser Settings

Use the various options of the browser menu to make better use of the web browser. The Menu icon (the three vertical bars in the upper-right corner of the Chrome window) lists a number of useful options for the Chrome browser. The following illustration shows the menu choices that appear when you open the browser menu.

If you select the Settings choice, a Settings screen appears with various settings used by the browser, as shown in the following illustration. You can use these settings to change various aspects of your browser's behavior, such as the search engine used by default and whether web forms are automatically filled in; options to accept or clear cookie data and whether to allow popups; and assorted advanced options which include whether the JavaScript programming language is enabled.

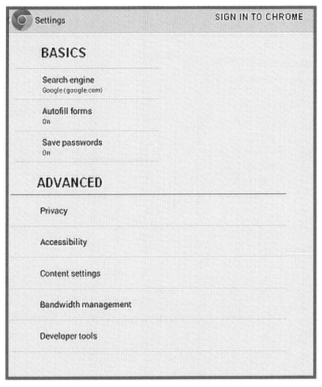

Tap Search Engine, and you can choose from three possible options : Google, Yahoo, and Microsoft's Bing. You can turn on the Autofill Forms option to enable the automatic filling in of web-based form fields that contain repetitive data, such as your name and address. The Saved Password option, when enabled, causes the Chrome browser to save passwords needed for access to password-proteccted websites.

Under the privacy settings, you can turn on or off suggestions for how navigation errors are handled, and you can control whether Chrome keeps track of usage and crash reports.

The Accessibility screen has a single option with you may find useful. Under Accessibility, you can adjust the Font Scaling property to make fonts larger or smaller until they are readable for you. Once in Chrome, tap the Settings icon at the upper right to display the Settings screen, then under the 'Advanced' category, tap Accessibility. At the next screen (see the following illustration), move the Text Scaling slider as needed to adjust the size of the text.

There are also a number of options under the Content Settings choice. You can choose whether or not to accept cookies data from other websites, whether or not to enable JavaScript, whether or not to block pop ups, whether you should allow websites to access your built-in microphone and camera for voice and video calling, and whether Google is able to use location-based services. Finally, under Bandwidth Management, you will see an option to pre-load web pages (this option, which is on by default, speeds up Chrome's general operations but it may do so at the expense of some pages not being as current as they could be.)

Using Bookmarks

As mentioned earlier in the chapter, bookmarks are an excellent way to quickly revisit websites that you visit on a regular basis. Rather than memorizing long and convoluted web addresses, you can easily bookmark web sites within Chrome. And Chrome makes it easy to bookmark sites, and to manage your bookmarks

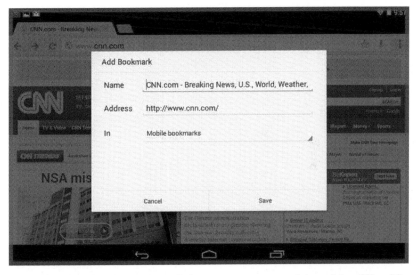 **Bookmark commonly visited pages so you can return to them quickly at a later time.** To add a bookmark, once at the page you want to bookmark, tap the Add Bookmark icon near the upper right corner of the web browser (it's the one in the shape of a star). When you do so, an Add Bookmark dialog box appears, similar to the example shown here.

Change the name of the entry to something friendlier if you desire, and tap Save, to add the page to your bookmarked pages.

When you open a new tab, you can tap the Menu icon, then choose Bookmarks from the menu that opens, to display a list of all of your bookmarked pages. Tap the desired bookmark to open that webpage.

Delete unwanted bookmarks. Tap the Menu icon, then choose Bookmarks from the menu that opens, to display a list of all of your bookmarked pages. You can then delete any bookmark by performing a long-press on the unwanted bookmark, and choosing "Delete Bookmark" from the menu that appears.

Add your extremely favored bookmarks directly to your home page. If there's a web site that you are really, really fond of, you can place a bookmark to that site directly on your home screen. Tap the Menu icon, then choose Bookmarks from the menu that opens, to display a list of all of your bookmarked pages. Perform a long-press on the desired bookmark, and choose "Add to Home screen" from the menu that appears.

Handy Web Browsing Tips

The "thumb and finger spread" or "thumb and finger pinch" works in the Chrome web browser. You will often encounter web pages with text that is too small to read on the tablet's screen. Place your thumb and finger on the screen and spread them to magnify, or pinch them together to reduce the magnification.

Use "Find on this page" as a search tool.
Oftentimes you will need to search a website for a particular
word or phrase. To do this in the web browser, tap the Menu
icon, then tap "Find on page." Enter a search term in the search
field that appears, and all instances of the term will be
highlighted within the text of the web page. A narrow scroll
area will also appear at the right side of the web browser, and
you can tap the highlighted portions within this scroll area to
move through the search results.

Let the browser complete your entry. As
you begin typing characters into the search / address field, a
list of suggestions appears below the field, based upon your
previous entries in the browser. If you see a suggestion that
matches the URL you intended to type, tap that suggestion.

Chapter 7: Multimedia Tips, Tricks, and Traps

As an entertainment device, your tablet is designed to work seamlessly with content that you purchase from the Google PlayStore. But, be warned that you are missing out on a wealth of other available content (much of it free) if you aren't familiar with ways to move compatible files from another source onto your tablet.

In addition to purchasing content from the Google PlayStore, you can find a wealth of content from other sources, and these can be copied to your tablet from your computer using the USB cable that is a part of your charging assembly. Android tablets use the popular E-PUB format used by Sony and by Google for e-books, and e-books in this format can be found in thousands of places all over the internet, some paid, and others free. There are also millions of books in the Amazon Kindle file format, and there are free converters readily available from hundreds of sources on the web that will convert files from the format used by all Amazon Kindles into the E-PUB format used by your tablet. Chapter 4 has the full details on this topic.

Transferring Content between a Computer and your tablet

You can use the same USB cable techniques to copy MP3, AAC, or WAV files that you obtain from your own sources, and these become a part of the music library on your tablet. There are apps like Crackle that let you stream any one of thousands of free movies or TV shows to your tablet. If you are already a Netflix subscriber, you can use the Netflix app (the app comes with the default apps on your tablet) and watch any content that you would normally obtain from Netflix. And short length, personal movies compatible with the tablet (in 3gp or mp4 format) can also be copied to the device, although memory size limitations are by nature going to limit the length of movies that can be stored locally on the device. (While you can and probably should add a microSD ram card to your tablet—if your tablet has such an expansion slot, see the tip later in this chapter in how to do this-- a single average Blu-ray DVD occupies 25 gigabytes of disk space.)

To take full advantage of all of these features, you'll need to know how to use the file transfer features of your tablet. You'll find the various tips, tricks, and traps that pertain to these topics covered throughout this chapter.

You can transfer files from a laptop or desktop computer to your tablet, using your power charger cable. This is the same cable that is supplied as a charging cable for your tablet; one end contains the connector that plugs into the base of your tablet, and the other end contains a standard USB connector. Use the cable to connect your tablet to your computer, and the tablet will appear as a USB flash drive under your computer's operating system. If you are using a Windows-based computer, you may see an "AutoPlay" dialog box (see below) when you initially connect the USB connector to your computer. If you see this dialog box, double-click the "Open Device to view files" option.

Once the tablet appears as a USB drive under your computer's operating system, you can simply drag and drop or copy and paste the desired files into the appropriate folders of the tablet. The following illustration shows the folders of a tablet when viewed as a flash drive on a Windows-based computer; the appearance is similar on a Mac.

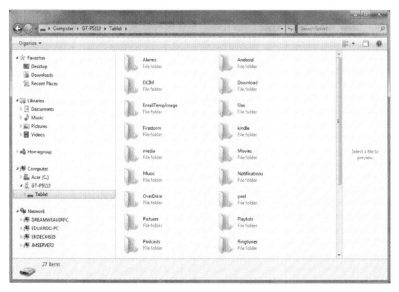

Three folders that you'll want to notice are the **Pictures** folder, the **Music** folder, and the **Movies** folder. Images that you copy into the Pictures folder from other sources (such as a digital camera) will appear as pictures in the Gallery app of the tablet. You can copy .MP3 files into the Music folder and play these using the Music Player. And video files can be copied into the Movies folder. These can also be played using the Gallery app.

As far as file formats are concerned, nearly all Android tablets support the following file formats:

-eBooks: ePub (Adobe Digital Rights Management, and non-Digital Rights Management files), PDF, CBZ

-Other documents: PDF, TXT

-Music: MP3, MP4, WAV, WMA, AAC, 3GP

-Videos: MP4, M4V, 3GP, AVI, MKV

-Pictures/Images: JPEG (JPG), GIF, PNG, or BMP

Using the Gallery to play videos

 Play your personal videos on your tablet. You can transfer video files or download video files and play them on your tablet. You can then use the Gallery app to play those videos. Use the previously-mentioned procedures to copy your movie files into the Movies folder that appears as part of the flash drive window when your tablet is connected to your computer. Once you've copied the file(s) to your tablet, go to your Apps screen and tap the Gallery icon (shown here) to open the Gallery.

The Gallery of a tablet is arranged as a series of tiles, similar to the example shown in the following illustration.

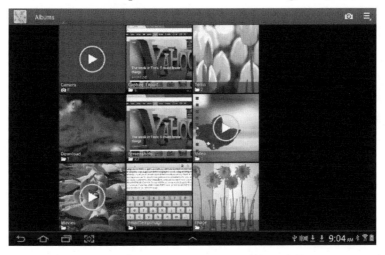

Tap the Movies tile, and you will see tiles representing each of your movies. Tap the desired movie to open it in a full screen, and tap the "Play" triangle that appears in the center of the screen to begin playing your movie. Once the movie begins playing, you can tap anywhere on the screen to display a series of video playback controls that include fast forward, rewind, play/pause, and volume and movie position sliders, as shown in the following illustration.

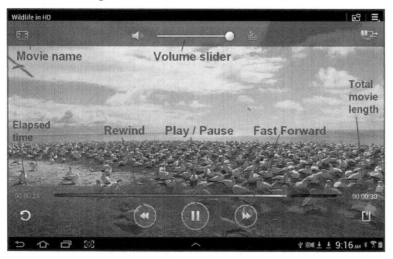

You can copy files that are stored in the video formats listed at the start of this chapter into the Movies folder that appears in the directory of folders shown on your computer when the tablet is connected by means of the USB cable. When you connect your tablet to the matching connector on one end of the charging cord and connect the standard USB side of the cable to your computers' USB port, the tablet appears on your computer's File Explorer or file management system as a USB flash drive. You can then use standard cut / copy / paste or drag-and-drop procedures to copy the video file into the Movies folder of your tablet, as described in the previous tip.

A file may exist in one of the acceptable file formats of 3GP or MP4, yet may refuse to play on a tablet. Not only must the files be stored in one of the acceptable formats, the length by width and video bitrate must fall within acceptable parameters, or the video will fail to play. You can use a conversion program on a desktop or laptop computer to convert video files such as your vacation movies shot with a DV camcorder to a format that will play on your tablet. Some digital camcorders use a DIV/X or AVI file format that may not play on a tablet without being converted to a format that is compatible with the tablet. (There is a solution to this issue; see the next tip.)

Converting Video Files to the tablet formats

If you have access to a Windows-based computer, you can use free video conversion software to convert video files to tablet formats using the steps we've outlined here.

1. Download a video converter software program for your PC. There are a number of programs that you can find with a Google search. While there are many that charge a fee, you can also find free converters. One that we give instructions for here is the "Any Video Converter, Free Edition." You can find it at http://www.any-video-converter.com/download-avc-free.php. *NOTE: When you install the program, at one point you will be asked "Standard Installation" or "Custom Installation." The Standard Installation will install an aftermarket toolbar and will modify the search options on your computer; if you don't want this to happen, change the option to "Custom Installation" and turn off both options listed when asked.*

2. Once the 'Any Video Converter, Free Edition' is installed on your computer launch the program, and when it opens, drag a video file that you want to convert to tablet format onto the main window of the program.

3. Click the Preset Output button at the upper right. A 'Choose your output device' appears, similar to the following illustration:

4. Scroll through the top of the list, and locate the tablet category.

5. Open the drop-down list of output formats immediately below the list of devices, and choose "tablet MPEG-4 Movie (*.mp4)" from the list.

6. In the "Save To" list box, select the file location on your computer where the file should be saved.

7. Click CONFIRM.

8. At the upper-right, click the "Convert All File(s) NOW" button. The file conversion process will begin, and as the file is converted, a progress bar will display the approximate time remaining for the conversion process.

9. When the conversion process has completed, you can copy the converted file to your tablet using the USB cable and the

file transfer procedures described earlier in this chapter. Copy the file into the Movies folder, and you can play it with the Gallery app listed among your default apps.

You can read Microsoft Office files on your tablet. Files created in Microsoft Office versions 97 through 2013, in Word, Excel, or PowerPoint, can be opened and read on your tablet. You can edit these files using apps that are designed to work with Microsoft Office files. One such app, Polaris Office, is supplied with the default apps installed on your tablet, and there are dozens of others available through the Google PlayStore (open the PlayStore, and search the 'Apps' category on the phrase 'microsoft office.')

Adding file storage space with a Micro SD Ram Card

With some models of tablets, you can increase the available storage space for personal files by adding an optional 4GB, 8GB, 16GB, or 32GB micro SD RAM card to your tablet. The addition of a micro SD RAM card will provide plenty of room for space-consuming items like personal videos or thousands of .mp3 music files. Tablets that have micro SD RAM slots support the use of micro SDHC cards of up to 64GB in size. If the card has been used previously in some other device (such as an Android phone), you will need to reformat the card using the Windows FAT file formatting system. You can do this from the Settings screen of your tablet once the card is inserted. You can also format a previously-used card by inserting the card into a standard SDram card adapter, inserting the adapter into your Windows laptop or desktop SD ram slot, and using Windows Explorer to format the card.

You can add a micro SD ram card using the following steps:

1. Completely power down your tablet by pressing and holding the power button for 10 seconds. When the turn off power prompt appears on the screen, tap power off.

2. Place your tablet face down on a cushioned surface, and determine where the micro SD Ram slot is located on your model of tablet. On certain tablets, the micro SD Ram slot is located on the edge that is opposite of the edge with the rear-facing camera, as shown here:

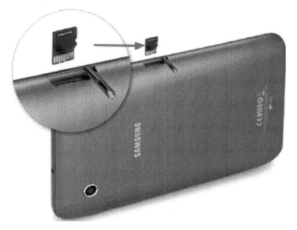

With some models, the micro SD RAM Slot is located on the edge closest to the rear-facing camera, as shown here:

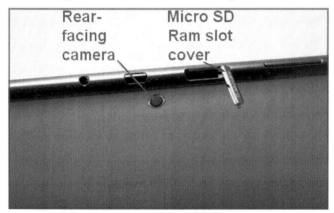

In nearly all cases, the slot is clearly labeled with the phrase, 'micro SD' or 'micro SD Ram'.

With a third type of tablet design, you will need to remove the rear cover of the device to access the SD ram card expansion slot. (Be sure to refer to your tablet's documentation for additional instructions if you have this type of tablet; the author of this book assumes no liability for your attempting to remove a device cover that was never intended for removal!!!)

3. Assuming your tablet uses a clearly-labeled card slot, locate the small protective cover over the micro SD card slot. Using your finger tip, **<u>gently</u>** pull the cover open, turning it to one side to reveal the slot, as shown in the previous illustration.

4. Hold the memory card gently between your thumb and forefinger, with the logo facing the front (screen side) of the tablet. Gently guide the card into the slot.

5. Push gently against the card, guiding it into the slot until it clicks into place.

6. Close the protective cover and snap it into place.

7. Power up your tablet, and then tap the Settings icon to get to your settings screen.

8. When the Settings screen appears, scroll down to Storage, and tap Mount SD Card, then tap Format SD Card. Confirm the operation when asked.

Once you've inserted a micro SD ram memory card into your tablet, when you examine the file structure of your tablet using a File Manager app, you will see a choice both for your tablet and for your memory card.

If you add an SD Ram card to increase the storage capacity of your tablet, get familiar with the File Manager app supplied with your default apps, or add another third-party file management app to your apps collection. Your tablet will automatically scan and display media content in the gallery and music apps you use, but if you want to access the files and folders directly, you must work with a file management app There are a number of file management apps available for your tablet, and many of these apps provide more flexibility and added capabilities over the File Manager app that comes with most tablets. This author likes ES File Explorer due to its flexibility and its clear, consistent user interface. If you're interested, search the Google PlayStore under 'Apps' for the search term "ES File Explorer."

Note that apps and any custom images that you plan to use for wallpapers or screen savers cannot be saved to a tablet's micro SD ram card; these must be saved to the internal memory of the tablet itself.

Adding cloud storage with Google Drive

You can increase the available storage space for personal files by making use of Google Drive with your Android tablet. Google Drive is a free service, provided by Google, that lets you store files that you create or view on your Android tablet online, in the cloud. Google Drive also provides access to Google Docs, a set of web-based apps that you can use to create documents, spreadsheets and other files online. Whenever you save files to Google Drive, your files are stored on web servers via the Internet, and these web servers are maintained by Google. Using Google Drive, you can access your files whether they are stored on your Android tablet, your android based smart phone, or your personal computer.

A big advantage of Google Drive is the shared synchronization aspect of all of your files. That trip itinerary on your Android tablet, that presentation at work, those recipes, that great American novel you've been writing in your

94

free time, and all those videos or photos that you took on that last cruise vacation- with Google Drive, you can get to all of those files from anywhere, as long as you can get to an internet connection.

And forget about files being too large to send by way of email. With Google Drive, you can share your files with others, even those large video files from your camcorder that are far too big to send as an attachment to an email message. Share your files with others, and everyone you choose to share your files with will be able to open, view, and (if you choose to allow this) edit those files. Google Drive allows true collaboration, so that multiple people can work on the same document at the same time.

Google Drive gives you 5 gigabytes of storage space where you can store files of different types. You can store two general types of files in Google Drive: ones that you can edit, and ones that you cannot edit. You can edit many types of files directly within Google Drive. These include documents, spreadsheets, and presentations in Google Docs format, Microsoft Office Word and Excel files, and text based files. Files that you cannot edit within Google Drive include music and video files. While those can't be edited it in Google Drive, you can store your music and video files on Google Drive.

Installing Google Drive

To use Google Drive easily, you'll want to install the Google Drive app, which is free. Open the Google Play Store on your Android tablet, and search for Google Drive. Download and install the app, and it will appear as an icon within your collection of apps.

While you are at the Google Play Store, you'll want to install a good file manager app if you plan to upload files from your Android tablet for use with Google Drive. This author highly recommends the ES File Explorer app, which is also free. Do a search in the Play Store on ES File Explorer File Manager, and download and install that app as well.

Using Google Drive

From the apps screen, tap the Google Drive icon (shown here) to launch Google Drive.

If you are using Google Drive for the first time, the window that appears will be empty, similar to the example shown in the illustration that follows. You'll want to note the plus symbol at the upper right, as shown in the illustration. This is the Create icon for Google Drive.

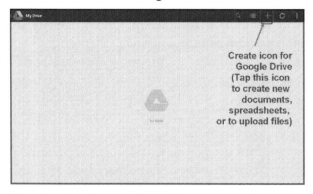

Create icon for Google Drive (Tap this icon to create new documents, spreadsheets, or to upload files)

Tap the plus icon and you'll see an Add New menu with choices for folder, document, spreadsheet, or upload. Tap document, and you will be asked to give the new document a name. Give the document a name and tap OK, and a window into the word processor for Google Docs will open. (If you are familiar with the use of Microsoft Word or Open Office Word for word processing, you will find the overall operation of the Google Docs word processor to be similar.) Alternately, you can tap the plus sign and when the Add New menu appears, tap spreadsheet, and you will be asked for a name for the new spreadsheet. Give it a name and tap OK, and a window into the spreadsheet application for Google Docs will open.

If you have music, video, or other types of files that you have uploaded to your Android tablet using the cable method described earlier in this book, and you want to transfer those files to Google Drive, you can easily do so. Tap the plus sign, and in the menu that appears choose Upload. The next menu that appears will give you a choice of upload options, and if you installed ES File Explorer, one of those choices within the menu will be ES File Explorer. Tap the ES File Explorer icon, and tap Always Use for this action, then tap OK. ES File Explorer will launch, and you can navigate to the folder on your Android tablet that contains the files you want to upload. Tap the desired file, then choose 'Normal' in the dialog box that appears to begin the file transfer.

Once you have added a number of files to your Google Drive, they appear in a tiled layout, similar to the example shown in the following illustration. You can open any of your files by simply opening Google Drive and tapping on the tile that represents the file that you wish to open.

Remember that you can get to your files stored in Google Drive from any personal computer. Just open a web browser on your personal computer, and go to **http://drive.google.com**. Log in with your Google account, and your Google Drive will appear, with all of your files.

Learn more about Google Drive and Google Docs with Google's instructional videos on YouTube. Google Drive and Google Docs make for one powerful combination, with Google Drive offering cloud-based storage for your files, and Google Docs providing full-powered web apps for creating word processing documents, spreadsheets, and presentations. Entire books have been written on this subject. But since YouTube happens to be a division of Google, the parent company has a series of YouTube videos that go into more detail on the use of Google Drive and Google Docs. To locate these instructional videos, point your browser at www.youtube.com and in the YouTube search box, enter the phrase 'learn Google Docs' or 'learn Google Drive.'

Chapter 8: Email Tips, Tricks, and Traps

One of the many capabilities of your tablet centers around the email client that is built into the device. All of the basic features that you would expect to find in an email client are here; you can open and read mail, reply to and compose mail, download attachments, and send email with attached files. Setting up e-mail accounts—on your tablet or on any computer—can be tricky, so we've included detailed instructions for e-mail setup and basic e-mail operation in this chapter. Tips, tricks, and traps dealing with email are also covered in this chapter.

Creating an E-Mail Account

Newer Android tablets have an e-mail setup application that automatically configures the required background settings for many types of e-mail. When setting up a new e-mail account on your tablet, try the automated setup first. Perform the following steps to set up an e-mail account on the tablet:

1. Tap the Apps icon ▦ to get to your Apps screen.

2. If this is your first e-mail account on your tablet, tap Gmail Ⓜ (to set up a Google account), or tap E-mail ✉ (to set up any other type of account). If you've already set up an e-mail account and want to add another, tap your Settings icon, and under "Accounts", tap Add Account, and choose the account type (corporate/Exchange, Google, POP3, or IMAP) that you wish to add.

3. Enter your email address and password associated with your account, and tap Next.

4. Give your account a name and enter a name to be displayed on your outgoing messages.

5. Tap Done. The Auto-configuration feature will set up your e-mail account, and you'll see your existing messages for the account in an e-mail window, similar to the example shown in the following illustration.

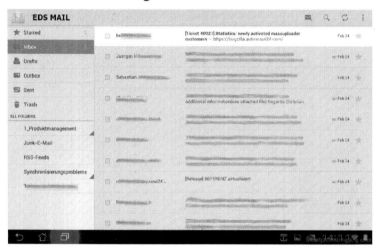

The auto configuration works with e-mail addresses that end in any of the following: @google.com, @hotmail.com, @mac.com, @me.com, @live.com, @yahoo.com, @yahoo.co.uk, @aim.com, @aol.com, @aol.co.uk, @android.com, @btinternet.com, @gmail.com, and @googlemail.com.

Setting Up tablet E-Mail Manually

The automated e-mail setup on the tablet does a great job when it works, but it does not always work, and when it fails to work, you'll need to set up your e-mail manually. (You will also need to perform a manual setup if you have an older tablet.) Before starting a manual e-mail account setup process, there is some information that you will want to make sure that you have from your e-mail service provider. Of course, you will need to know your e-mail address and the password for the account. In addition, you will need to know the server settings of your mail server. You will need the SMTP settings, as well as either the POP or the IMAP settings. (The SMTP setting is used for sending mail, and POP and IMAP are both used for receiving mail. IMAP is a newer standard for receiving mail, so if your mail server supports both POP and IMAP, use the IMAP settings.) Finally, you will need to know the security type used by the servers, and the default incoming and outgoing ports. (You should be able to obtain all of this information from your e-mail provider.) Once you've obtained the information, perform the following steps to set up an e-mail account on the tablet:

1. At the Home screen, tap Apps and then scroll to and tap Email. If you have not set up an account yet, an email setup screen will appear. (If you have already set up an email account, the E-mail app will open.) Note that on some models of Android tablets, to add another account first tap your Settings icon, then under "Accounts", tap Add Account, and choose the account type (corporate/Exchange, Google, POP3, or IMAP) that you wish to add..

2. Enter your Email address and password.

3. Tap Next, then tap Manual Setup to manually configure your connection settings.

4. Select the type of email account you are creating. (Your available choices are a POP3 account, an IMAP account, or a Microsoft Exchange ('corporate') account. These steps will help you with the common POP3 and IMAP types; if you are setting up a Microsoft Exchange-hosted account, contact your Exchange Administrator or hosting provider for the needed settings.)

5. Next, you will be asked to provide your incoming server settings. These will include your user name, password, POP3 or IMAP server address, security type, port number, and the desired 'delete email from server' setting. Enter this information, then tap Next.

Your tablet will attempt to connect to the Incoming server with the settings you supplied. If the connection is successful, the Outgoing server settings screen will appear.

6. Enter your outgoing server settings. These will include your user name, password, SMTP server address, security type (if any), port number, and whether the server will require a sign-in. After entering this information, tap Next.

The first time you connect, you will be asked to give this mail account a unique on-screen name, and you will need to supply your name. (The e-mail app uses the unique account name to differentiate the account from all other email accounts on your tablet.) Touch Done, and your manually created e-mail account is ready for use.

Reading Your Mail

You'll know when you have incoming mail on your tablet, because you'll see a notification icon in the form of an envelope with a red circle along one side or at the top or bottom edge of the Home screen, and unless you've silenced alerts, you'll hear a tone (the type of tone can be changed or silenced in Settings). If you get a new Gmail message, you see the New Gmail notification appear on the screen, and for any other type of mail, you see a new Email notification appear.

Tap the notification icon at the edge of the screen to view a summary of your most recent message. If there are multiple unread messages in your Inbox, there will be a number showing how many unread messages are in your Inbox.

To get to your Inbox, tap Apps then tap Gmail for a Google mail account), or tap Email (for all other accounts). Your Inbox opens, displaying your mail in a fashion similar to that shown here:

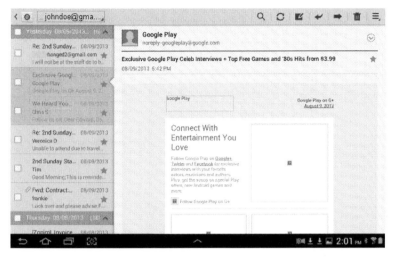

To read an e-mail, just open the Inbox containing your mail by choosing it by name in the Accounts list (if you have more than one account set up on your tablet.) Tap the desired mail item in the list to open the mail, and its content will appear in the active window.

Switching between multiple mail accounts

If you've set up more than one e-mail account, you can switch by tapping Account (at the top of the E-mail screen). Choose the inbox for the account you want to check.

The default Android e-mail app has a nice feature called the combined inbox, which displays mail from multiple accounts simultaneously. At the top of the Inbox screen, tap the drop-down list of mailboxes, and choose Combined Inbox from the list. Once you do this, you will see all messages from all established accounts within a single list.

Composing and Sending Mail

Writing email is also a straightforward process. At the Home screen tap Apps  then tap the Gmail icon to get into Gmail, or tap the E-Mail icon to get into the e-mail app.

Once in the e-mail app, tap the pencil icon in the upper-left corner. When you do so, a Compose Email window appears, similar to the following example.

Type an address in the To box. (Alternately, you can tap the Contacts icon and choose an address that's in your Contacts list. When entering multiple names, separate any additional names with commas. (You can also use the Cc: and Bcc: fields to add copied recipients and blind copied recipients, respectively.)

In the Subject area, enter a subject for the message, and then enter the desired message text in the Message area. You can add attachments (such as photos stored on your tablet) by tapping the Attachments icon (the one resembling a paper clip), navigating to the desired attachment, and tapping it to attach the file. When done, tap the Send icon to send the message.

Change the signature line. When you send mail using your tablet's Email app, the signature line, "Sent from my tablet." is appended onto the end of every message that you send. You can change this tagline to something more personable with these steps:

1. Open the tablet Email app, and get into the e-mail account that you wish to change the signature for.

2. Tap the Menu icon at the upper right corner of the screen and choose Settings.

3. Under General Preferences, tap the Signature option.

4, Change or delete the text in the dialog box that appears, and tap OK.

Using your synchronized calendars and contacts

Once you've set up your e-mail accounts, assuming that you allow synchronization of calendars and contacts with your e-mail accounts, you will also be able to use the Calendar and Contacts apps built into your Android tablet. At the Home screen, tap Apps, then tap Calendar. A view of a synchronized calendar from your Google, Microsoft, or Yahoo account will appear (the illustration that follows shows an example of a synchronized calendar based on a Google account).

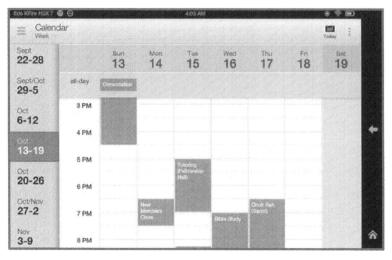

You can make changes or additions to your calendar by tapping within any date and time field, and then tapping the Plus (+) symbol that appears. A New Event screen will appear, and you can enter the details about your calendar event.

To see your synchronized contacts list, get to the Home screen, tap Apps, and locate and tap the Contacts icon. A synchronized contacts list will appear; the following illustration shows an example of a Contacts list based on a Google account. (And yes, the author does have a fondness for dead presidents, particularly the ones depicted on greenbacks, but that is another story.)

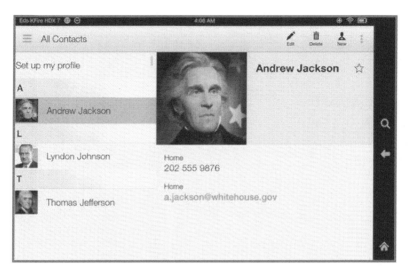

When viewing any contact, you can use the toolbar buttons that appear at one edge of the screen to edit an existing contact in your list, to delete a contact, or to add a new contact. As with the calendar, since the accounts are synchronized with those of your e-mail provider, any changes that you make using your tablet will be entered in the cloud-based contacts list provided by your e-mail provider.

Consider using an optional app as your Email client. While the Email client that is built into the tablet does an acceptable job, you should be aware that this is not your only option for managing email. There are apps available from the Google PlayStore, at least one of them free, which serve as perfectly acceptable alternatives to the tablet's built-in e-mail app. One that this author particularly likes is K-9 by K-9 Dog Walkers. K-9 is a free, open-source e-mail client that's available for the tablet. It supports IMAP, POP3, and Microsoft Exchange 2003 and 2007 (with WebDAV), supports multiple folders, and has full searching capabilities (something that the default e-mail client that comes with the tablet sadly lacks). Go to the Google PlayStore, and search on the term "k9 mail" to locate the K-9 app for the tablet.

Chapter 9: Camera Tips, Tricks, and Traps

IMPORTANT NOTE: This chapter details the use of built-in cameras provided with many, but not all, makes and models of tablets. If your model of tablet does not offer a built in camera, then your reading this chapter is pretty much a waste of your time, and you're welcome to skip to the chapter that follows.

Many tablets offer built-in cameras that you can put to use, whether it be for quick and impromptu snapping of still photos, filming those silly cat videos for uploading to YouTube, or conducting video phone calls with relatives who happen to be on the other side of the country (or the planet).

The bright, vivid screen on the typical tablet can be quite useful when showing off your photos to family and friends, but that is not all that's possible with your tablet. The built-in Gallery app also has the capability to do photo editing, and you can share your pictures via e-mail, instant messaging, or social networking apps such as Facebook.

Using the Camera App

You can use to the camera app that comes with the default apps provided on the tablet to take pictures or videos. On tablets with a single front-facing camera, your camera app will control that camera. On tablets equipped with both front and rear-facing cameras, the Camera app controls either of the two built-in cameras: typically a low resolution VGA camera that is front facing (or facing towards you when you are looking at the screen), and a high resolution camera that is rear-facing. To launch the Camera app, tap Home, then Apps, then tap the Camera icon. When you initially launch the Camera app, if your tablet has a micro SD ram slot and a micro SDram card is installed, you will be asked whether you want to change the storage settings for your photos and videos to the

SDram card. Click OK in the dialog box to change the storage location, or click Cancel to store your photos and videos in your tablet's internal memory.

When the Camera app loads, if your tablet has a single camera, you see a view presented by the front-facing camera. If your tablet has dual cameras, you see one of two views, depending on whether the camera app is set to use the front-facing or the rear-facing camera. At the left and right sides of the screen are the various controls of the Camera app, as shown in the following illustration. (Your exact set of controls and their location will vary depending on your model of Android tablet.)

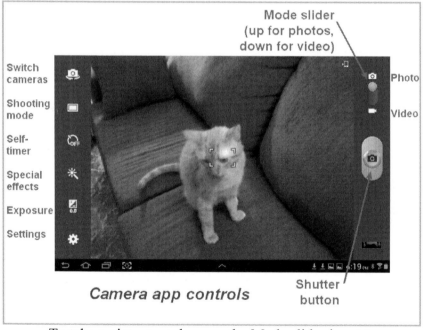

Camera app controls

To take a picture, make sure the Mode slider is set to Camera, point at and frame your subjects, and tap the Shutter icon. The camera will auto focus, and you'll hear a sound as the camera takes a photo.

tip! Immediately after taking a picture, a preview icon appears at the lower right corner of the Camera app. Tap the icon to see a preview of this photo you've taken. If you don't care for the photo and want to retake it, you can touch the trash can icon at the upper-right to delete the image, then use the Back icon at the lower left to get back into the Camera app.

Using the Camera Options

With most Android tablets, the shooting mode option offers you a variety of picture taking modes, including single shot (the default), panoramic view, buddy photo share, or smile shots. Use the self timer option when you want to add yourself to the photo. Tap Self timer, and you can choose between a 2 second, 5 second, or a 10 second delay before the picture is taken. Use the special effects tool to apply a special effect tinting to the overall photo. Your choices are black and white, sepia tone, or negative effect.

The exposure option lets you set the overall exposure (light or dark) of the photo, and the Settings icon displays a variety of camera settings that you can change, as shown in the following illustration.

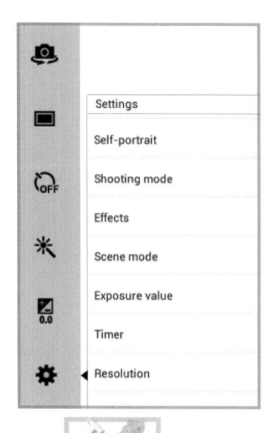

| Settings |
| Self-portrait |
| Shooting mode |
| Effects |
| Scene mode |
| Exposure value |
| Timer |
| ◄ Resolution |

Remember that if you use any of the special effects, such as black and white or negative, these are permanently applied to the selected photo. It may be a better idea to save the photo in the manner that it was taken, and then use a photo editing program to apply a special effect, and save the photo under a different name.

Using the Gallery App

Of course, being able to take photos is a fairly useless activity if you don't have a way to get to those photos. You can easily get to your photos by means of the Gallery app that is a default app in your tablet's collection of apps. To get there, from the Home screen, tap Apps, then tap the Gallery icon (shown here).

When you do this, the Gallery opens, and its content appears, similar to the example shown in the following illustration.

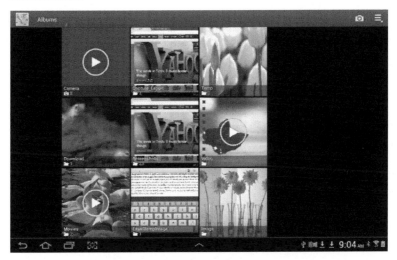

Your content within the Gallery is arranged by category. If you've taken any videos, or uploaded videos to your tablet using the cable method described in prior chapters, those will be displayed in the gallery as well. You can tap the camera tile within the Gallery to display all of your photos, then tap any photo to open that photo in a full screen view.

While the photo is open in a full screen view, you can tap the Share icon (the one that looks like a letter V spacing sideways) to open a menu of share options. You can share photos via e-mail, through Google's own Picassa photo-sharing service, with a nearby Bluetooth-equipped device (such as a printer, smartphone, or laptop computer with Bluetooth capability), or a number of other selections, depending upon what apps you have installed on your tablet. (The following illustration shows the share options that appear on the author's tablet; yours may differ, but the Bluetooth, Google+, Gmail, and Picassa options will appear on all machines.)

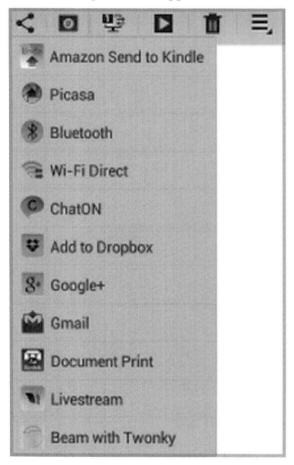

Finally, remember that if you have a Windows-based PC or an Apple Macintosh, you can copy the photo or video files taken with your tablet cameras to the hard drive of your personal computer, using the techniques described in chapter 7. (Refer to chapter 7 for further details on how to copy files.)

Chapter 10: Battery and Power Tips, Tricks, and Traps

The battery life of an Android tablet is respectable if not stellar, averaging five to ten hours of moderate video use, depending upon the model. But for those times when you may spend hours and hours away from an electrical outlet, there are specific tips that can help you get more out of your tablet's battery life and go for longer periods of time between charges.

Dim the screen, lengthen the battery life. Much of the power consumed by your tablet goes toward lighting that high definition screen, and the brighter the screen is lit, the more power that gets consumed. So when you're seated in that cramped tin can called an airliner at 30,000 feet, flying across the Pacific, turn down the brightness. To do this, tap your Settings icon, then under Device, tap Display. then Brightness. A slider will appear, and you can adjust the brightness down to a level that's comfortable for reading. (Your battery will last longer, and you can always turn the brightness back up after you're at the hotel in Honolulu!)

Adjust your screen timeout. By default, your tablet automatically dims its screen after a certain period of inactivity. You can adjust the time period, and the shorter the period, the longer your battery life. To do this, tap Settings, then under Device, tap Display. Tap Screen Timeout and set this to as short a time as you are comfortable with.

Shut down wi-fi when there's no chance of getting a wi-fi signal. In places where there is no chance of getting a working wi-fi signal (such as most commuter rail lines and most aircraft), the wireless circuitry inside your tablet doesn't know any better and stays unusually active, checking for a wi-fi signal and consuming an abnormally high amount of battery power. An easy way to prevent this is to disable the tablet's Wi-Fi. (You will still be able to access any content you've already downloaded, such as your music, most apps, and any books and personal videos that are stored on your device.) To do this, drag down from the top of the screen (or on some models, tap the clock in the Navigation bar to display the Quick Settings dialog box), and tap the Wi-Fi indicator to turn your wi-fi OFF. (When you are back in range of a strong wi-fi signal, remember to turn your wi-fi back on.)

On tablet models with built-in speakers, use earphones in place of the built in speakers. Most headphones and earphones use much less power than do the speakers that are built into the tablet.

Every so often, run down the battery to the 15% level on purpose. If you're the type of individual that keeps your rechargeable devices connected to a wall outlet, you may actually be shortening your battery life in the long run. The type of battery used by any Android tablet (as is used by other tablets and most laptop computers) actually loses its effectiveness over time if it is constantly kept in a state of near-full charge. The way to prevent this is to perform what is called a "deep discharge"—you intentionally allow your battery to run down closer to the point of exhaustion before

116

recharging your device. Every so often, allow the battery to discharge to the point where the "Low Battery Warning" indicator appears on the screen. Doing this on a monthly basis will help keep your tablet's battery working near top-notch condition.

Chapter 11: Accessories for your Android tablet

Your Android tablet may be a great tablet for the money, but there's generally not much in the box when you open it. You get the tablet itself, a USB charging cable and power adapter combination, and a quick start guide in the form of a few printed pages. Fortunately, the phenomenal popularity of tablet computers in general has resulted in a wide variety of accessories, and with a minimal amount of effort you can find a number of suppliers of those same accessories. Here, in no particular order, are various accessories that you may want to consider purchasing for your Android tablet.

(1) A protective case. These can be obtained in an incredible variety of styles and colors. If you have a 10-inch Android tablet, the well-known laptop carrying case manufacturer, Targus, offers **the Targus CityGear Mini case**, a durable and attractive case that accommodates any ten-inch tablet.

(Technically, this case will accommodate 7-inch Android tablets as well, but smaller tablets are somewhat dwarfed by the bag which was clearly made to accommodate larger tablets.) Besides having those nice internal side pouches where you can stuff various items (like business cards and breath mints,) the Targus CityGear Mini case retails for around twenty dollars from a number of retailers, including WalMart, Target Stores, Best Buy and many office supply retailers.

(2) A protective case that fits like a glove. If you prefer the type of case that's sized to fit your specific model of tablet, you'll find that close-fitting cases are in abundant supply. Amazon is a great source for made-to-fit tablet cases, and the easiest way to locate a case that fits your tablet is to go to Amazon's web site, click or tap in the Search box, and type the exact make and model of your tablet, followed by the word 'cases.' The resulting cases for your model of tablet will appear.

A note of caution: When choosing a tablet case sight unseen from the pages of the Amazon website (or that of any other mail-order retailer), pay attention to the customer reviews. There's a large assortment of quality cases for sale via mail-order, and unfortunately, there are also a number of cases of shoddy quality and poor construction. The customer reviews are an excellent means of determining the quality level of any case that you are considering.

Among the features you may want to look for when choosing a case are cases designed to wake or put your device to sleep by opening or closing the case, cases that secure the tablet with no straps (using a magnetic cover), and cases that sport a built-in stand to allow for hands-free viewing. Cases from most manufacturers also come in a variety of colors.

If you're seeking a close-fitting case that's easy on the wallet, case maker Fintie offers a durable polyurethane case for a number of 7-inch and 10-inch models of Android tablets. The company offers ready-to-fit cases for Google's Nexus 7, Samsung's Galaxy Tab 3, the Asus MeMO Pad, the Acer Iconia Tab, Barnes and Noble's NOOK, and both the 7-inch and 8.9-inch models of Amazon's Kindle Fire. At Amazon's web site, click or tap in the Search box, and enter the phrase 'Fintie cases for android tablets' to see a list of ready-to-fit cases offered by this particular manufacturer.

(3) A Power charger kit. I like the Nyko 3-In-One Power Kit, available from most WalMart stores or from WalMart's online store for two reasons: reasonable cost (just under $30 at the time of this writing), and flexibility. You get an AC adapter that's compatible with a majority of Android tablets, a car charger that plugs into your car or truck cigarette lighter for charging on the go, and a 3-foot long charging cable. One end of the cable inserts into either the wall adapter or the car charger adapter, and the other end plugs into the micro USB port used as a charging connector on most Android tablets.

(Nyko 3-In-One Power Kit from WalMart)

(4) A pillow to relax and curl up with a good tablet (pun on words intended): The **Accessory Workshop typillow** also comes from WalMart Online, costs roughly $33, is made from a soft monosuede material, and securely holds a 7-inch Android tablet in place while lounging.

the Accessory Workshop typillow

(5) A Case for Commuting. Big city commuters who use their tablets as a means of entertainment during those long commutes will like **Marware's Jumi Case** for the 7-inch Android tablet. Available from WalMart Online at a cost of around $30, the Jumi case by Marware comes in four different colors, and has a zippered compartment to accommodate cash, credit cards, and a farecard or rail pass. There's also a handy strap attached to the rear of the case that will accommodate one's hand, making this case ideal for performing the "one-handed read of the day's news" while your opposite hand is wrapped around a pole of a standing-room-only commuter rail car.

Jumi case for 7-inch Android tablets by Marware

(6) Ditch the soft keyboard. If your Android tablet has Bluetooth capability and you would like to use your machine for some serious typing (without inducing paralysis of the fingers due to the relatively small soft keyboard), consider a wireless Bluetooth keyboard. You turn on the keyboard, then go into **Settings > Wireless > Bluetooth** on your Android tablet, and choose the keyboard from a list of wireless Bluetooth devices in your area (this process is known as *pairing*). Once you've paired the keyboard with your tablet, the simple act of switching on power at the keyboard pairs the keyboard to your Android tablet, leaving you to touch-type to your heart's content. Bluetooth keyboards come in both portable and standard desktop computer sizes. They can be purchased from a number of sources, including Radio Shack, Best Buy, WalMart, and Amazon.

(7) **Android to go.** For those who spend their travel time behind the wheel (as opposed to riding a commuter train), there's the Tablet Cup Holder Mount by Bracketron.

Available through Amazon at a cost of around $25 at the time of this writing, the Bracketron Cup Holder Mount fits securely in one of the cup holders of your vehicle while providing a convenient, "hands free" location for your Android tablet. Search the Amazon web site for "Bracketron cup holder mount" (but please don't attempt to use your Android tablet while driving).

(8)- **Better sound.** Finally, the last recommended accessory is one that you likely already own. You're sure to increase the fidelity of the sound provided by any speakers that may be built into your tablet, with the addition of a reasonable-quality set of headphones or the addition of a set of external speakers.

CONCLUSION (and a favor to ask!)

I truly hope that you enjoy using your tablet as much as I have enjoyed using mine and writing about the tablet. As an author, I'd love to ask a favor: if you have the time, please consider writing a short review of this book. Honest reviews help me to write better books. You can post a review by going to the Amazon.com website, searching for the title "Android tablet tips, tricks and traps," scrolling to the bottom of the page that appears, and clicking the 'write a customer review' link. And my sincere thanks for your time!

Many think that tablets are just for checking e-mail, watching YouTube videos, and surfing the web, but they can do so much more. Hopefully, after you have had the opportunity to try some of the many tips and tricks that have been outlined in this guide, you'll discover that for yourself.

-Ed Jones

Join our mailing list...

We would be honored to add your name to our mailing list, where we can keep you informed of any book updates and of additional tips or topics about technology. Our mailing list will NEVER be sold to others (because we hate spam as much as you probably do), and the only information that we will ask you to supply is a valid e-mail address. Point your web browser at www.thekindlewizard.com and click the "Join our mailing list' link.

By the way, 'the kindle wizard' happens to be one of the author's aliases. If you or anyone in your family owns an Amazon Kindle, you may wish to check out the numerous articles and resources on the site. The password that you'll need for the 'book owners' portion of the site is *kindle4ever*.

Other books by the author: To visit the author's Amazon page for a complete list of books, point your web browser to the following address:

`www.amazon.com/author/edwardjones_writer`

Alternately, visit the author's website at www.thekindlewizard.com.

Android Tablet Tips, Tricks, and Traps:

A How-To Tutorial for all Android Tablets

Edward Jones

13773173R00072

Printed in Great Britain
by Amazon.co.uk, Ltd.,
Marston Gate.